PEARSON   ALWAYS LEARNING

Edited by Kathleen Callahan Martin

Readings in Social Theory & Modernization

Spring 2017

Boston University College of General Studies

Pearson Education, Inc., 330 Hudson Street, New York, New York 10013
A Pearson Education Company
www.pearsoned.com

Printed in the United States of America

1   16

000200010272014212

JHA/KS

ISBN 10: 1-323-61089-8
ISBN 13: 978-1-323-61089-3

Copyright Acknowledgments

Contents

From Leviathan 1
  Thomas Hobbes

The Social Contract 5
  Jean Jacques Rousseau

From Second Treatise of Civil Government 15
  John Locke

The Declaration of Independence 19

The Declaration of the Rights of Man and Citizen 23

The Declaration of the Rights of Woman 27
  Olympe de Gouges

Justification of the Use of Terror 33
  Maximilien Robespierre

The World We Have Lost 37
  Peter Laslett

From The Sadler Report 47

Exploitation 55
  E. P. Thompson

On Liberty 61
  John Stuart Mill

Nations and Nationalism 71
  Heinrich von Treitschke

Imperialism, the Latest Stage of Capitalism 77
  V.I. Lenin

Confession of Faith 85
  Cecil Rhodes

On the Democratic Welfare State 89
    Franklin D. Roosevelt

The Social Bases of Nazism 93
    David Schoenbaum

The Doctrine of Fascism 107
    Benito Mussolini

Think About What You Saw: The Holocaust and Social Science 111
    John W. Mackey

Concerning Violence 123
    Frantz Fanon

Nonviolent Power in Action 127
    Dennis Dalton

Why Can't People Feed Themselves? 133
    Frances Moore Lappé and Joseph Collins

Globalization and Inequality 143
    Joseph Stiglitz

The New Global American Dilemma and Terrorism 153
    Fathali M. Moghaddam

From *Leviathan*

Thomas Hobbes

An Oxford educated mathematician, Hobbes (1588–1679) is best known for Leviathan, *one of the world's most influential works on political theory. This book, published in 1651 during an era of political and social turmoil, argued that rational persons could best attain order and security by agreeing to the formation of a social contract, a new and radical idea at the time. Under such an arrangement, he said, citizens would willingly surrender some of their freedom in exchange for the safety that a powerful sovereign ruler could give them.*

Of the Natural Condition of Mankind as Concerning Their Felicity and Misery

Men by nature equal. Nature hath made men so equal, in the faculties of the body, and mind; as that though there be found one man sometimes manifestly stronger in body, or of quicker mind than another; yet when all is reckoned together, the difference between man, and man, is not so considerable, as that one man can thereupon claim to himself any benefit, to which another may not pretend, as well as he. For as to the strength of body, the weakest has strength enough to kill the strongest, either by secret machination, or by confederacy with others, that are in the same danger with himself.

From equality proceeds diffidence. From this equality of ability, ariseth equality of hope in the attaining of our ends. And therefore if any two men desire the same thing, which nevertheless they cannot both enjoy, they become enemies and in the way to their end, which is principally their own conservation, and sometimes their delectation only, endeavour to destroy, or subdue one another. And from hence it comes to pass, that where an invader hath no more to fear, than another man's single power; if one plant, sow, build, or possess a convenient seat, others may probably be expected to come prepared with forces united, to dispossess, and deprive him, not only of the fruit of his labour, but also of his life, or liberty. And the invader again is in the like danger of another.

So that in the nature of man, we find three principal causes of quarrel. First, competition; secondly, diffidence; thirdly, glory.

The first, maketh men invade for gain; the second, for safety; and the third, for reputation. The first use violence, to make themselves masters of other men's persons, wives, children, and cattle; the second, to defend them; the third, for trifles, as a word, a smile, a different opinion, and any other sign of undervalue, either direct in their persons, or by reflection in their kindred, their friends, their nation, their profession, or their name.

Out of civil states, there is always war of every one against every one. Hereby it is manifest, that during the time men live without a common power to keep them all in awe, they are in that condition which is called war; and such a war, as is of every man, against every man. For WAR, consisteth not in battle only, or the act of fighting; but in a tract of time, wherein the will to contend by battle is sufficiently known: and therefore the notion of *time,* is to be considered in the nature of war; as it is in the nature of weather. For as the nature of foul weather, lieth not in a shower or two of rain; but in an inclination thereto of many days together: so the nature of war, consisteth not in actual fighting; but in the known disposition thereto, during all the time there is no assurance to the contrary. All other time is PEACE.

The incommodities of such a war. Whatsoever therefore is consequent to a time of war, where every man is enemy to every man; the same is consequent to the time, wherein men live without other security, than what their own strength, and their own invention shall furnish them withal. In such condition, there is no place for industry; because the fruit thereof is uncertain: and consequently no culture of the earth; no navigation, nor use of the commodities that may be imported by sea; no commodious building; no instruments of moving, and removing, such things as require much force; no knowledge of the face of the earth; no account of time; no arts; no letters; no society; and which is worst of all, continual fear, and danger of violent death; and the life of man, solitary, poor, nasty, brutish, and short.

Of the First and Second Natural Laws, and of Contracts

Right of nature what. The RIGHT OF NATURE, which writers commonly call *jus naturale,* is the liberty each man hath, to use his own power, as he will himself, for the preservation of his own nature; that is to say, of his own life; and consequently, of doing any thing, which in his own judgment, and reason, he shall conceive to be the aptest means thereunto.

Liberty what. By LIBERTY, is understood, according to the proper signification of the word, the absence of external impediments: which impediments, may oft take away part of a man's power to do what he would; but cannot hinder him from using the power left him, according as his judgment, and reason shall dictate to him.

A law of nature what. Difference of right and law. A LAW OF NATURE, *lex naturalis,* is a precept or general rule, found out by reason, by which a man is forbidden to do that, which is destructive of his life, or taketh away the means of preserving the same; and to omit that, by which he thinketh may be best preserved. For though they that speak of this subject, use to confound *jus,* and *lex, right* and *law:* yet they ought to be distinguished; because RIGHT, consisteth in liberty to do, or to forbear: whereas LAW, determineth, and bindeth to one of them: so that law, and right, differ as much, as obligation, and liberty; which in one and the same matter are inconsistent.

Naturally every man has right to every thing. The fundamental law of nature. And because the condition of man, as hath been declared in the precedent chapter, is a condition of war of every one against every one; in which case every one is governed by his own reason; and there is nothing he can make use of, that may not be a help unto him, in preserving his life against his enemies; it followeth, that in such a condition, every man has a right to every thing; even to one another's body. And therefore, as long as this natural right of every man to every thing endureth, there can be no security to any man, how strong or wise soever he be, of living out the time, which nature ordinarily alloweth men to live. And consequently it is a precept, or general rule of reason, *that every man, ought to endeavour peace,* as far as he has hope of *obtaining it; and when he cannot obtain it, that he may seek, and use, all helps, and advantages of war.* The first branch of which rule, containeth the first, and fundamental law of nature; which is, *to seek peace, and follow it.* The second, the sum of the right of nature; which is, *by all means we can, to defend ourselves.*

Of the Causes, Generation, and Definition of a Commonwealth

The end of commonwealth, particular security. The final cause, end, or design of men, who naturally love liberty, and dominion over others, in the introduction of that restraint upon themselves, in which we see them live in commonwealths, is the foresight of their own preservation, and of a more contented life thereby; that is to say, of getting themselves out from that miserable condition of war, which is necessarily consequent, as hath been shown (chapter 15), to the natural passions of men, when there is no visible power to keep them in awe, and tie them by fear of punishment to the performance of their covenants, and observation of those laws of nature set down in the fourteenth and fifteenth chapters.

Which is not to be had from the law of nature. For the laws of nature, as *justice, equity, modesty, mercy,* and, in sum, *doing to others, as we would be done to,* of themselves, without the terror of some power, to cause them to be observed, are contrary to our natural passions, that carry us to partiality, pride, revenge, and the like. And covenants, without the sword, are but words, and of no strength to secure a man at all. Therefore notwithstanding the laws of nature (which every one hath then kept, when he has the will to keep them, when he can do it safely) if there be no power erected, or not great enough for our security; every man will, and may lawfully rely on his own strength and art, for caution against all other men. And in all places, where men have lived by small families, to rob and spoil one another, has been a trade, and so far from being reputed against the law of nature, that the greater spoils they gained, the greater was their honour; and men observed no other laws therein but the laws of honour; that is, to abstain from cruelty, leaving to men their lives, and instruments of husbandry. And as small families did then; so now do cities and kingdoms which are but greater families, for their own security, enlarge their dominions, upon all pretences of danger, and fear of invasion, or assistance that may be given to invaders, and endeavour as much as they can, to subdue, or weaken their neighbours, by open force, and secret arts, for want of other caution, justly; and are remembered for it in after ages with honour.

For if we could suppose a great multitude of men to consent in the observation of justice, and other laws of nature, without a common power to keep them all in awe; we might as well suppose all mankind to do the same; and then there neither would be, nor need to be any civil government, or commonwealth at all; because there would be peace without subjection.

The generation of a commonwealth. The definition of commonwealth. The only way to erect such a common power, as may be able to defend them from the invasion of foreigners, and the injuries of one another, and thereby to secure them in such sort, as that by their own industry, and by the fruits of the earth, they may nourish themselves and live contentedly; is, to confer all their power and strength upon one man, or upon one assembly of men, that may reduce all their wills, by plurality of voices, unto one will; which is as much as to say, to appoint one man, or assembly of men, to bear their person; and every one to own, and acknowledge himself to be author of whatsoever he that so beareth their person, shall act, or cause to be acted, in those things which concern the common peace and safety; and therein to submit their wills, every one to his will, and their judgments, to his judgment. This is more than consent, or concord; it is a real unity of them all, in one and the same person, made by covenant of every man with every man, in such manner, as if every man should say to every man, *I authorize and give up my right of governing myself, to this man, or to this assembly of men, on this condition, that thou give up thy right to him, and authorize all his actions in like manner.* This done, the multitude so united in one person, is called a COMMONWEALTH, in Latin CIVITAS. This is the generation of that great LEVIATHAN, or rather, to speak more reverently, of that *mortal god,* to which we owe under the *immortal God,* our peace and defence. For by this authority, given him by every particular man in the commonwealth, he hath the use of so much power and strength conferred on him, that by terror thereof, he is enabled to form the wills of them all, to peace at home, and mutual aid against their enemies abroad. And in him consisteth the essence of the commonwealth; which, to define it, is *one person, of whose acts a great multitude, by mutual covenants one with another, have made themselves every one the author, to the end he may use the strength and means of them all, as he shall think expedient, for their peace and common defence.*

Sovereign, and subject, what. And he that carrieth this person is called SOVEREIGN, and said to have *sovereign power;* and every one besides, his SUBJECT.

The attaining to this sovereign power, is by two ways. One by natural force; as when a man maketh his children, to submit themselves, and their children to his government, as being able to destroy them if they refuse; or by war subdueth his enemies to his will, giving them their lives on that condition. The other, is when men agree amongst themselves, to submit to some man, or assembly of men, voluntarily, on confidence to be protected by him against all others. This latter, may be called a political commonwealth, or commonwealth by *institution;* and the former, a commonwealth by *acquisition.* And first, I shall speak of a commonwealth by institution.

The Social Contract

Jean Jacques Rousseau

Jean-Jacques Rousseau (1712–1778) was a Genevan-born Frenchman who first attained fame as an essayist in Paris, and who quarreled bitterly and publicly with many other leading French Enlightenment figures. During the French Revolution, the ideas contained in his Social Contract *became wildly popular and greatly influenced revolutionary leaders, especially Jacobin leaders such as Maximilien Robespierre.*

Book 1: Chapter 1: Subject of the First Book

Man is born free; and everywhere he is in chains. One thinks himself the master of others, and still remains a greater slave than they. How did this change come about? I do not know. What can make it legitimate? That question I think I can answer. If I took into account only force, and the effects derived from it, I should say: "As long as a people is compelled to obey, and obeys, it does well: as soon as it can shake off the yoke, and shakes it off, it does still better; for, regaining its liberty by the same right as took it away, either it is justified in resuming it, or there was no justification for those who took it away." But the social order is a sacred right which is the basis of all other rights. Nevertheless, this right does not come from nature, and must therefore be founded on conventions. Before coming to that, I have to prove what I have just asserted. . . .

Book 1: Chapter 3: The Right of the Strongest

The strongest is never strong enough to be always the master, unless he transforms strength into right, and obedience into duty. Hence the right of the strongest, which, though to all seeming meant ironically, is really laid down as a fundamental principle. But are we never to have an explanation of this phrase? Force is a physical power, and I fail to see what moral effect it can have. To yield to force is an act of necessity, not of will—at the most, an act of prudence. In what sense can it be a duty?

Suppose for a moment that this so-called "right" exists. I maintain that the sole result is a mass of inexplicable nonsense. For, if force creates right, the effect changes with the cause: every force that is greater than the first succeeds to its right. As soon as it is possible to disobey with impunity, disobedience is legitimate; and, the strongest being always in the right, the only thing that matters is to act so as to become the strongest. But what kind of right is that which perishes when force fails? If we must obey perforce, there is no need to obey because we ought; and if we are not forced to obey, we are under no obligation to do so. Clearly, the word "right" adds nothing to force: in this connection, it means absolutely nothing.

Obey the powers that be. If this means yield to force, it is a good precept, but superfluous: I can answer for its never being violated. All power comes from God, I admit; but so does all sickness: does that mean that we are forbidden to call in the doctor? A brigand surprises me at the edge of a wood: must I not merely surrender my purse on compulsion; but, even if I could withhold it, am I in conscience bound to give it up? For certainly the pistol he holds is also a power.

Let us then admit that force does not create right, and that we are obliged to obey only legitimate powers. In that case, my original question recurs.

Book 1: Chapter 4: Against Slavery

. . . To renounce liberty is to renounce being a man, to surrender the rights of humanity and even its duties. For him who renounces everything no indemnity is possible. Such a renunciation is incompatible with man's nature; to remove all liberty from his will is to remove all morality from his acts. Finally, it is an empty and contradictory convention that sets up, on the one side, absolute authority, and, on the other, unlimited obedience. Is it not clear that we can be under no obligation to a person from whom we have the right to exact everything? Does not this condition alone, in the absence of equivalence or exchange, in itself involve the nullity of the act? For what right can my slave have against me, when all that he has belongs to me, and, his right being mine, this right of mine against myself is a phrase devoid of meaning?

Grotius and the rest find in war another origin for the so-called right of slavery. The victor having, as they hold, the right of killing the vanquished, the latter can buy back his life at the price of his liberty; and this convention is the more legitimate because it is to the advantage of both parties. But it is clear that this supposed right to kill the conquered is by no means deducible from the state of war. Men, from the mere fact that, while they are living in their primitive independence, they have no mutual relations stable enough to constitute either the state of peace or the state of war, cannot be naturally enemies. War is constituted by a relation between things, and not between persons; and, as the state of war cannot arise out of simple personal relations, but only out of real relation, private war, or war of man with man, can exist neither in the state of nature, where there is no constant property, nor in the social state, where everything is under the authority of the laws.

Individual combats, duels and encounters, are acts which cannot constitute a state; while the private wars, authorized by the Establishments of Louis IX, King of France, and suspended by the Peace of God, are abuses of feudalism, in itself an absurd system if ever there was one, and contrary to the principles of natural right and to all good polity.

War then is a relation, not between man and man, but between State and State, and individuals are enemies only accidentally, not as men, nor ever as citizens, but as soldiers; not as members of their country, but as its defenders. Finally, each State can have for enemies only other States, and not men; for between things disparate in nature there can be no real relation. . . .

Book 1: Chapter 6: The Social Contract

I suppose men to have reached the point at which the obstacles in the way of their preservation in the state of nature show their power of resistance to be greater than the resources at the disposal of each individual for his maintenance in that state. That primitive condition can then subsist no longer; and the human race would perish unless it changed its manner of existence.

But, as men cannot engender new forces, but only unite and direct existing ones, they have no other means of preserving themselves than the formation, by aggregation, of a sum of forces great enough to overcome the resistance. These they have to bring into play by means of a single motive power, and cause to act in concert.

This sum of forces can arise only where several persons come together: but, as the force and liberty of each man are the chief instruments of his self-preservation, how can he pledge them without harming his own interests, and neglecting the care he owes to himself? This difficulty, in its bearing on my present subject, may be stated in the following terms:

"The problem is to find a form of association which will defend and protect with the whole common force the person and goods of each associate, and in which each, while uniting himself with all, may still obey himself alone, and remain as free as before." This is the fundamental problem of which the Social Contract provides the solution.

The clauses of this contract are so determined by the nature of the act that the slightest modification would make them vain and ineffective; so that, although they have perhaps never been formally set forth, they are everywhere the same and everywhere tacitly admitted and recognized, until, on the violation of the social compact, each regains his original rights and resumes his natural liberty, while losing the conventional liberty in favor of which he renounced it.

These clauses, properly understood, may be reduced to one—the total alienation of each associate, together with all his rights, to the whole community; for, in the first place, as each gives himself absolutely, the conditions are the same for all; and, this being so, no one has any interest in making them burdensome to others.

Moreover, the alienation being without reserve, the union is as perfect as it can be, and no associate has anything more to demand: for, if the individuals retained certain rights, as there would be no common superior to decide between them and the public, each, being on one point his own judge, would ask to be so on all; the state of nature would thus continue, and the association would necessarily become inoperative or tyrannical.

Finally, each man, in giving himself to all, gives himself to nobody: and as there is no associate over whom he does not acquire the same right as he yields others over himself, he gains an equivalent for everything he loses, and an increase of force for the preservation of what he has.

If then we discard from the social compact what is not of its essence, we shall find that it reduces itself to the following terms—

"Each of us puts his person and all his power in a common agreement under the supreme direction of the general will, and, in our corporate capacity, we receive each member as an indivisible part of the whole."

At once, in place of the individual personality of each contracting party, this act of association creates a moral and collective body, composed of as many members as the assembly contains votes, and receiving from this act its unity, its common indemnity, its life and its will. This public person, so formed by the union of all other persons formerly took the name of city, and now takes that of Republic or body politic; it is called by its members State when passive, Sovereign when active, and Power when compared with others like itself. Those who are associated in it take collectively the name of people, and severally are called citizens, as sharing in the sovereign power, and subject, as being under the laws of the State. But these terms are often confused and taken one for another: it is enough to know how to distinguish them when they are being used with precision.

Book 1: Chapter 7: The Sovereign

This formula shows us that the act of association comprises a mutual undertaking between the public and the individuals, and that each individual, in making a contract, as we may say, with himself, is bound in a double capacity; as a member of the Sovereign, he is bound to the individuals, and as a member of the State to the Sovereign. But the maxim of civil law that no one is bound by undertakings made to himself, does not apply in this case; for there is a great difference between incurring an obligation to yourself and incurring one to a whole of which you form a part.

Attention must further be called to the fact the public deliberation, while competent to bind all the subjects to the Sovereign, because of the two different capacities in which each of them may be regarded, cannot, for the opposite reason, bind the Sovereign to itself; and that it is consequently against the nature of the body politic for the Sovereign to impose on itself a law which it cannot infringe. Being able to regard itself in only one capacity, it is in the position of an individual who makes a contract with himself; and this makes it clear that there neither is nor can be any kind of fundamental law binding on the body of the people—not even the social contract itself. This does not mean that the body politic cannot enter into undertakings with others, provided the contract is not infringed by them; for in relation to what is external to it, it becomes a simple being, an individual.

But the body politic or the Sovereign, drawing its being wholly from the sanctity of the contract, can never bind itself, even to an outsider, to do anything derogatory to the original act, for instance to alienate any part of itself, or to submit to another Sovereign. Violation of the act by which it exists would be self-annihilation; and that which is itself nothing can create nothing.

As soon as this multitude is so united in one body, it is impossible to offend against one of the members without attacking the body, and still more to offend against the body without the members resenting it. Duty and interest therefore equally oblige the two contracting parties to give each other help; and the same men should seek to combine, in their double capacity, all the advantages dependent upon that capacity.

Again, the Sovereign, being formed wholly of the individuals who compose it, neither has nor can have any interest contrary to theirs; and consequently the sovereign power need give no guarantee to its subject, because it is impossible for the body to wish to hurt all its members. We shall also see later on that it cannot hurt any in particular. The Sovereign, merely by virtue of what it is, is always what it should be.

This, however, is not the case with the relation of the subjects to the Sovereign, which, despite the common interest, would have no security that they would fulfill their undertakings, unless it found means to assure itself of their fidelity.

In fact, each individual, as a man, may have a particular will contrary or dissimilar to the general will which he has as a citizen. His particular interest may speak to him quite differently from the common interest: his absolute and naturally independent existence may make him look upon what he owes to the common cause as a gratuitous contribution, the loss of which will do less harm to others than the payment of it is burdensome to himself; and, regarding the moral person which constitutes the State as a *persona ficta*, because to a man, he may wish to enjoy the rights of citizenship without being ready to fulfill the duties of a subject. The continuance of such an injustice could not but prove the undoing of the body politic.

In order then that the social compact may not be an empty formula, it tacitly includes the undertaking, which alone can give force to the rest, that whoever refuses to obey the general will shall be compelled to do so by the whole body. This means nothing less than that he will be forced to be free; for this is the condition which, by giving each citizen to his country, secures him against all personal dependence. In this lies the key to the working of the political machine; this alone legitimizes civil undertakings, which, without it, would be absurd, tyrannical, and liable to the most frightful abuses.

Book 1: Chapter 8: The Civil State

The passage from the state of nature to the civil state produces a very remarkable change in man, by substituting justice for instinct in his conduct, and giving his actions the morality they formerly lacked. Then only, when the voice of duty takes the place of physical impulses and right of appetite, does man, who so far had considered only himself, find that he is forced to act on different principles, and to consult his reason before listening to his inclinations. Although, in this state, he deprives himself of some advantages which he got from nature, he gains in return others so great, his faculties are so stimulated and developed, his ideas so extended, his feelings so ennobled, and his whole soul so uplifted, that, did not the abuses of this new condition often degrade him below that which he left, he would be bound to bless continually the happy moment which took him from it for ever, and, instead of a stupid and unimaginative animal, made him an intelligent being and a man.

Let us draw up the whole account in terms easily commensurable. What man loses by the social contract is his natural liberty and an unlimited right to everything he tries to get and succeeds in getting; what he gains is civil liberty and the proprietorship of all he possesses. If we are to avoid mistake in weighing one against the other, we must clearly distinguish natural liberty, which is bounded only by the strength of the individual, from civil liberty, which is limited by the general will; and possession, which is merely the effect of force or the right of the first occupier, from property which can be founded only on a positive title.

We might, over and above all this, add, to what man acquires in the civil state, moral liberty, which alone makes him truly master of himself; for the mere impulse of appetite is slavery, while obedience to a law which we prescribe to ourselves is liberty. But I have already said too much on this head, and the philosophical meaning of the word liberty does not now concern us.

Book 1: Chapter 9: Real Property

. . . I shall end . . . this book by remarking on a fact on which the whole social system should rest: i.e. that, instead of destroying natural inequality, the fundamental compact substitutes, for such physical inequality as nature may have set up between men, an equality that is moral and legitimate, and that men, who may be unequal in strength or intelligence, become every one equal by convention and legal right.

Book 2: Chapter 1: The Sovereignty Is Inalienable

The first and most important deduction from the principles we have so far laid down is that the general will alone can direct the State according to the object for which it was instituted, i.e., the common good: for if the clashing of particular interests made the establishment of societies necessary, the agreement of these very interests made it possible. The common element in these different interests is what forms the social tie; and, were there no point of agreement between them all, no society could exist. It is solely on the basis of this common interest that every society should be governed.

I hold then that Sovereignty, being nothing less than the exercise of the general will, can never be alienated, and that the Sovereign, who is no less than a collective being, cannot be represented except by himself: the power indeed may be transmitted, but not the will.

In reality, if it is not impossible for a particular will to agree on some point with the general will, it is at least impossible for the agreement to be lasting and constant; for the particular will tends, by its very nature, to partiality, while the general will tends to equality. It is even more impossible to have any guarantee of this agreement for ever if it should always exist, it would be the effect not of art, but of chance. The Sovereign may indeed say: "I now will actually what this man wills, or at least what he says he wills"; but it cannot say: "What he wills tomorrow, I too shall will" because it is absurd for the will to bind itself for the future, nor is it incumbent on any will to consent to anything that is not for the good of the being who wills. If then the people promises simply to obey, by that very act it dissolves itself and loses what makes it a people; the moment a master exists, there is no longer a Sovereign, and from that moment the body politic has ceased to exist.

This does not mean that the commands of the rulers cannot pass for general wills, so long as the Sovereign, being free to oppose them, offers no opposition. In such a case, universal silence is taken to imply the consent of the people. This will be explained later on.

Book 2: Chapter 2: The Sovereignty Is Indivisible

Sovereignty, for the same reason as makes it inalienable, is indivisible; for will either is, or is not, general; it is the will neither of the body of the people, nor only of a part of it. In the first case, the will, when declared, is an act of Sovereignty and constitutes law: in the second, it is merely a particular will, or act of magistracy—at the most a decree.

But our political theorists, unable to divide Sovereignty in principle, divide it according to its object: into force and will; into legislative power and executive power; into rights of taxation, justice and war; into internal administration and power of foreign treaty. Sometimes they confuse all these sections, and sometimes they distinguish them; they turn the Sovereign into a fantastic being composed of several connected pieces: it is as if they were making man of several bodies, one with eyes, one with arms, another with feet, and each with nothing besides. We are told that the jugglers of Japan dismember a child before the eyes of the spectators; then they throw all the members into the air one after another, and the child falls down alive and whole. The conjuring tricks of our political theorists are very like that; they first dismember the body politic by an illusion worthy of a fair, and then join it together again we know not how.

This error is due to a lack of exact notions concerning the Sovereign authority, and to taking for parts of it what are only emanations from it. Thus, for example, the acts of declaring war and making peace have been regarded as acts of Sovereignty; but this is not the case, as these acts do not constitute law, merely the application of a law, a particular act which decides how the law applies, as we shall see clearly when the idea attached to the word law has been defined. . . .

Book 2: Chapter 3: Whether the General Will Is Fallible

It follows from what has gone before that the general will is always right and tends to the public advantage; but it does not follow that the deliberation of the people are always equally correct. Our will is always for our own good, but we do not always see what that is; the people is never corrupted, but is often deceived, and on such occasions only does it seem to will what is bad.

There is often a great deal of difference between the will of all and the general will; the latter considers only the common interest, while the former takes private interest into account, and is not more than a sum of particular wills: but take away from these same wills the pluses and minuses that cancel one another, and the general will remains as the sum of the differences.

If, when the people, being furnished with adequate information, held its deliberations, the citizens had no communication one with another, the grand total of the small differences would always give the general will, and the decision would always be good. But when fractions arise, and partial associations are formed at the expense of the great association, the will of each of these associations becomes general in relation to its members, while it remains particular in relation to the State: it may then be said that there are no longer as many votes as there are men, but only as many as there are associations. The differences become less numerous and give a less general result. Lastly, when one of these associations is so great as to prevail over all the rest, the result is no longer a sum of small differences, but a single difference; in this case there is no longer a general will, and the opinion which prevails is purely particular.

It is therefore essential, if the general will is to be able to express itself, that there should be no partial society within the State, and that each citizen should think only his own thought which was indeed the sublime and unique system established by the great Lycurgus. But if there are partial societies, it is best to have as many possible and to prevent them from being unequal, as was done by Solon, Numa and Servius. These precautions are the only ones that can guarantee that the general will shall be always enlightened, and that the people shall in no way deceive itself.

Book 2: Chapter 4: The Limits of the Sovereign Power

If the state is a moral person whose life is in the union of its members, and if the most important of its cares is the care of its own preservation, it must have a universal and compelling force, in order to move and dispose each part as may be most advantageous to the whole. As nature gives each man absolute power over all his members, the social compact gives the body politic absolute power over all its members also; and it is this power which, under the direction of the general will, bears, as I have said, the name of Sovereignty.

But, besides the public person, we have to consider the private persons composing it, whose life and liberty are naturally independent of it. We are bound then to distinguish clearly between the respective rights of the citizens and the Sovereign, and between the duties the former have to fulfill as subjects, and the natural rights they should enjoy as men.

Each man alienates, I admit, by the social compact, only such part of his powers, goods and liberty as it is important for the community to control; but it must also be granted that the Sovereign is sole judge of what is important.

Every service a citizen can render the State he ought to render as soon as the Sovereign demands it; but the Sovereign, for its part, cannot impose upon its subjects any fetters that are useless to the community, nor can it ever wish to do so; for no more by the law of reason than by the law of nature can anything occur without a cause.

The undertakings which bind us to the social body are obligatory only because they are mutual; and their nature is such that in fulfilling them we cannot work for others without working for ourselves. Why is it that the general will is always in the right, and that all continually will the happiness of each one, unless it is because there is not a man who does not think of "each" as meaning him, and consider himself in voting for all? This proves that equality of rights and the idea of justice which such equality creates originate in the preference each man gives to himself, and accordingly in the very nature of man. It proves that the general will, to be really such, must be general in its object as well as its essence; that it must both come from all and apply to all; and that it loses its natural rectitude when it is directed to some particular and determinate object, because in such a case we are judging of something foreign to us, and have no true principle of equity to guide us.

Indeed, as soon as a question of particular fact or right arises on a point not previously regulated by a general convention, the matter becomes contentious. It is a case in which the individuals concerned are one party, and the public the other, but in which I can see neither the law that ought to be followed nor the judge who ought to give the decision. In such a case, it would be absurd to propose to refer the question to an express decision of the general will, which can be only the conclusion reached by one of the parties and in consequence will be, for the other party, merely an external and particular will, inclined on this occasion to injustice and subject to error. Thus, just as a particular will cannot stand off for the general will, the general will, in turn, changes its nature, when its object is particular, and, as general, cannot pronounce on a man or a fact. When, for instance, the people of Athens nominated or displaced its rulers, decreed honors to one, and imposed penalties on another, and, by a multitude of particular decrees, exercised all the functions of government indiscriminately, it had in such cases no longer a general will in the strict sense; it was acting no longer as Sovereign, but as magistrate. This will seem contrary to current views; but I must be given time to expound my own.

It should be seen from the foregoing that what makes the will general is less the number of voters than the common interest uniting them; for, under this system, each necessarily submits to the conditions he imposes on others: and this admirable agreement between interest and justice gives to the common deliberations an equitable character which at once vanishes when any particular question is discussed, in the absence of a common interest to unite and identify the ruling of the judge with that of the party.

From whatever side we approach our principle, we reach the same conclusion, that the social compact sets up among the citizens an equality of such a kind, that they all bind themselves to observe the same conditions and should therefore all enjoy the same rights. Thus, from the very nature of the compact, every act of Sovereignty, i.e. every authentic act of the general will, binds or favors all the citizens equally; so that the Sovereign recognizes only the body of the nation, and draws no distinctions between those of whom it is made up. What, then strictly speaking, is an act of Sovereignty? It is not a convention between the body and each of its members. It is legitimate, because based on the social contract, and equitable, because common to all; useful, because it can have no other object than the general good, and stable, because guaranteed by the public force and the supreme power. So long as the subjects have to submit only to conventions of this sort, they obey no one but their own will; and to ask how far the respective rights of the Sovereign and the citizens extend, is to ask up to what point the latter can enter into undertakings with themselves, each with all, and all with each.

We can see from this that the sovereign power, absolute, sacred and inviolable as it is, does not and cannot exceed the limits of general conventions, and that every man may dispose at will of such goods and liberty as these conventions leave him; so that the Sovereign never has a right to lay more charges on one subject than on another, because, in that case, the question becomes particular, and ceases to be within its competency.

When these distinctions have once been admitted, it is seen to be so untrue that there is, in the social contract, any real renunciation on the part of the individuals, that the position in which they find themselves as a result of the contract is really preferable to that in which they were before. Instead of a renunciation, they have made an advantageous exchange: instead of an uncertain and precarious way of living they have got one that is better and more secure; instead of natural independence they have got liberty, instead of power to harm others' security for themselves, and instead of their strength, which others might overcome, a right which social union makes invincible. Their very life, which they have devoted to the State, is by it constantly protected; and when they risk it in the State's defence, what more are they doing than giving back what they have received from it? What are they doing that they would not do more often and with greater danger in the state of nature, in which they would inevitably have to fight battles at the peril of their lives in defence of that which is the means of their preservation? All have indeed to fight when their country needs them; but then no one has ever to fight for himself. Do we not gain something by running, on behalf of what gives us our security, only some of the risks we should have to run for ourselves, as soon as we lost it?

Book 2: Chapter 6: Law

I . . . give the name "Republic" to every State that is governed by laws, no matter what the form of its administration may be: for only in such a case does the public interest govern, and the *res publica* rank a reality. Every legitimate government is republican; what government is I will explain later on.

Laws are, properly speaking, only the conditions of civil association. The people, being subject to the laws, ought to be their author: the conditions of the society ought to be regulated solely by those who come together to form it. But how are they to regulate them? Is it to be by common agreement by a sudden inspiration? Has the body politic an organ to declare its will? Who can give it the foresight to formulate and announce its acts in advance? Or how is it to announce them in the hour of need? How can a blind multitude, which often does not know what it wills, because it rarely knows what is good for it, carry out for itself so great and difficult an enterprise as a system of legislation? Of itself the people wills always the good, but of itself it by no means always sees it. The general will is always in the right, but the judgement which guides it is not always enlightened. It must be got to see objects as they are, and sometimes as they ought to appear to it; it must be shown the good road it is in search of, secured from the seductive influences of individual wills, taught to see times and spaces as a series, and made to weigh the attractions of present and sensible advantages against the danger of distant and hidden evils. The individuals see the good they reject; the public wills the good it does not see. All stand equally in need of guidance. The former must be compelled to bring their wills into conformity with their reason; the latter must be taught to know what it wills. If that is done, public enlightenment leads to the union of understanding and will in the social body: the parts are made to work exactly together, and the whole is raised to its highest power. This makes a legislator necessary.

From *Second Treatise of Civil Government*

John Locke

*John Locke is regarded by many as both the first major Enlightenment figure
and as the father of modern democracy. An ardent supporter of William of
Orange, who became king of England in 1688 during the Glorious Revolution,
Locke published* The Second Treatise *shortly after William's accession to the
throne. In it, he outlined the case for a more rational, responsive type of
monarchy—a constitutional monarchy—that was designed to protect the
"natural rights" of citizens as its primary responsibility. In this work, Locke
directly rebuts many of the earlier ideas of Thomas Hobbes.*

I think it may not be amiss to set down what I take to be political power; that the
power of a magistrate over a subject may be distinguished from that of a father over
his children, a master over his servants, a husband over his wife, and a lord over his
slave. All which distinct powers happening sometimes together in the same man, if
he be considered under these different relations, it may help us to distinguish these
powers one from another, and show the difference betwixt a ruler of a commonwealth, a father of a family, and a captain of a galley.

Political power, then, I take to be a right of making laws with penalties of death
and, consequently, all less penalties for the regulating and preserving of property,
and of employing the force of the community in the execution of such laws, and
in the defence of the commonwealth from foreign injury, and all this only for the
public good.

Of the State of Nature

To understand political power right, and derive it from its original, we must consider
what state all men are naturally in, and that is a state of perfect freedom to order their
actions and dispose of their possessions and persons as they think fit, within the bounds
of the law of nature, without asking leave or depending upon the will of any other man.

A state also of equality, wherein all the power and jurisdiction is reciprocal, no
one having more than another; there being nothing more evident than that creatures

of the same species and rank, promiscuously born to all the same advantages of nature and the use of the same faculties, should also be equal one amongst another without subordination or subjection. . . .

But though this be a state of liberty, yet it is not a state of license. . . . The state of nature has a law of nature to govern it which obliges every one; and reason, which is that law, teaches all mankind who will but consult it that, being all equal and independent, no one ought to harm another in his life, health, liberty, or possessions; for men being all the workmanship of one omnipotent and infinitely wise Maker—all the servants of one sovereign master, sent into the world by his order, and about his business—they are his property whose workmanship they are, made to last during his, not one another's, pleasure; and being furnished with like faculties, sharing all in one community of nature, there cannot be supposed any such subordination among us that may authorize us to destroy another, as if we were made for one another's uses as the inferior ranks of creatures are for ours. . . .

Of Property

Whether we consider natural reason, which tells us that men, being once born, have a right to their preservation, and consequently to meat and drink and such other things as nature affords for their subsistence; or revelation, which gives us an account of those grants God made of the world to Adam, and to Noah and his sons; it is very clear that God, as King David says (Psal. cxv. 16), "has given the earth to the children of men," given it to mankind in common. . . . But this being supposed, it seems to some a very great difficulty how any one should ever come to have a property in anything. . . .

Though the earth and all inferior creatures be common to all men, yet every man has a property in his own person; this nobody has any right to but himself. The labour of his body and the work of his hands, we may say, are properly his. Whatsoever then he removes out of the state that nature hath provided and left it in, he hath mixed his labour with, and joined to it something that is his own, and thereby makes it his property. . . . Thus this law of reason makes the deer that Indian's who hath killed it; it is allowed to be his goods who hath bestowed his labour upon it, though before it was the common right of every one. . . . As much land as a man tills, plants, improves, cultivates, and can use the product of, so much is his property. . . . God gave the world to men in common; but since he gave it them for their benefit and the greatest conveniences of life they were capable to draw from it, it cannot be supposed he meant it should always remain common and uncultivated. He gave it to the use of the industrious and rational—and labour was to be his title to it—not to the fancy or covetousness of the quarrelsome and contentious.

Of the Beginning of Political Societies

Men being, as has been said, by nature all free, equal, and independent, no one can be put out of this estate and subjected to the political power of another without his own consent. The only way whereby any one divests himself of his natural liberty, and puts on the bonds of civil society, is by agreeing with other men to join and unite into a community for their comfortable, safe, and peaceable living one amongst another, in a secure enjoyment of their properties and a greater security against any that are not of it. This any number of men may do, because it injures not the freedom of the rest; they are left as they were in the liberty of the state of nature. When any number of men have so consented to make one community or government, they are thereby presently incorporated and make one body politic wherein the majority have a right to act and conclude the rest. . . .

Of the Ends of Political Society and Government

If man in the state of nature be so free, as has been said, if he be absolute lord of his own person and possessions, equal to the greatest, and subject to nobody, why will he part with his freedom, why will he give up his empire and subject himself to the dominion and control of any other power? To which it is obvious to answer that though in the state of nature he hath such a right, yet the enjoyment of it is very uncertain and constantly exposed to the invasion of others; for all being kings as much as he, every man his equal, and the greater part no strict observers of equity and justice, the enjoyment of the property he had in this state is very unsafe, very unsecure. This makes him willing to quit a condition which, however free, is full of fears and continual dangers; and it is not without reason that he seeks out and is willing to join in society with others who are already united, or have a mind to unite, for the mutual preservation of their lives, liberties, and estates, which I call by the general name "property."

The great and chief end, therefore, of men's uniting into commonwealths and putting themselves under government is the preservation of their property.

Of the Dissolution of Government

The reason why men enter into society is the preservation of their property; and the end why they choose and authorize a legislative is that there may be laws made and rules set as guards and fences to the properties of all the members of the society, to limit the power and moderate the dominion of every part and member of the society; for since it can never be supposed to be the will of the society that the legislative should have a power to destroy that which every one designs to secure by entering into society, and for which the people submitted themselves to legislators of their own making, whenever the legislators endeavour to take away and destroy the property of the people, or to reduce them to slavery under arbitrary power, they put themselves into a state of war with the people who are thereupon absolved from any further obedience, and are left to the common refuge which God hath provided for all men against force and violence. Whensoever, therefore, the legislative shall transgress this fundamental rule of society, and either by ambition, fear, folly, or corruption, endeavour to grasp themselves, or put into the hands of any other, an absolute power over the lives, liberties, and estates of the people, by this breach of trust they forfeit the power the people had put into their hands for quite contrary ends, and it devolves to the people who have a right to resume their original liberty, and by the establishment of a new legislative, such as they shall think fit, provide for their own safety and security, which is the end for which they are in society.

The Declaration of Independence

(As it reads in the parchment copy)

The Unanimous Declaration of the Thirteen United States of America

When in the Course of human events, it becomes necessary for one people to dissolve the political bands, which have connected them with another, and to assume among the powers of the earth, the separate and equal station to which the Laws of Nature and of Nature's God entitle them, a decent respect to the opinions of mankind requires that they should declare the causes which impel them to the separation. We hold these truths to be self-evident, that all men are created equal, that they are endowed by their Creator with certain unalienable Rights, that among these are Life, Liberty and the pursuit of Happiness. That to secure these rights, Governments are instituted among Men, deriving their just powers from the consent of the governed. That whenever any Form of Government becomes destructive of these ends, it is the Right of the People to alter or to abolish it, and to institute new Government, laying its foundation on such principles and organizing its powers in such form, as to them shall seem most likely to effect their Safety and Happiness. Prudence, indeed, will dictate that Governments long established should not be changed for light and transient causes; and accordingly all experience hath shewn, that mankind are more disposed to suffer, while evils are sufferable, than to right themselves by abolishing the forms to which they are accustomed. But when a long train of abuses and usurpations, pursuing invariably the same Object evinces a design to reduce them under absolute Despotism, it is their right, it is their duty, to throw off such Government, and to provide new Guards for their future security. Such has been the patient sufferance of these Colonies; and such is now the necessity which constrains them to alter their former Systems of Government. The history of the present King of Great Britain is a history of repeated injuries and usurpations, all having in direct object the establishment of an absolute Tyranny over these States. To prove this, let Facts be submitted to a candid world. He has refused his Assent to Laws, the most wholesome and necessary for the public good. He has forbidden his Governors to pass Laws of immediate and pressing importance, unless suspended in their operation till his Assent should be obtained; and when so suspended, he has utterly neglected to attend to them. He has refused to pass other Laws for the accommodation of large districts of people, unless those people would relinquish the right of Representation in the Legislature, a right inestimable to them and formidable to tyrants only. He has called together legislative bodies at places unusual, uncomfortable, and distant from the depository of their public Records, for the sole purpose of fatiguing them into compliance with his measures. He has dissolved Representative Houses repeatedly, for opposing with manly firmness his invasions on the rights of the people. He has refused for a long time, after such dissolutions, to cause others to be elected; whereby the Legislative powers, incapable of Annihilation, have returned to the People at large for their exercise; the State remaining in the meantime exposed to all the dangers of invasion from without, and convulsions within. He has endeavoured to prevent the population of these States; for that purpose obstructing the Laws for Naturization of Foreigners; refusing to pass others to encourage their migrations hither, and raising the condition of new appropriations of Lands. He has obstructed the Administration of Justice, by refusing his Assent to Laws for establishing Judiciary powers. He has made Judges dependent on his Will alone, for the tenure of their offices, and the amount and payment of their salaries. He has erected a multitude of New Offices, and sent hither swarms of Officers to harass our people, and eat out their substance. He has kept among us, in times of peace, Standing Armies without the Consent of our legislatures. He has affected to render the Military independent of and superior to the Civil power. He has combined with others to subject us to a jurisdiction foreign to our constitution, and unacknowledged by our laws; giving his Assent to their Acts of pretended Legislation. For quartering large bodies of armed troops among us: For protecting them, by a mock Trial, from punishment for any Murders which they should commit on the Inhabitants of these States: For cutting off our Trade with all parts of the world: For imposing Taxes on us without our Consent: For depriving us in many cases, of the benefits of Trial by Jury: For transporting us beyond Seas to be tried for pretended offenses: For abolishing the free System of English Laws in a neighboring Province, establishing therein an Arbitrary government, and enlarging its Boundaries so as to render it at once an example and fit instrument for introducing the same absolute rule into these Colonies: For taking away our Charters, abolishing our most valuable Laws, and altering fundamentally the Forms of our Governments: For suspending our own Legislatures, and declaring themselves invested with power to legislate for us in all cases whatsoever. He has abdicated Government here, by declaring us out of his Protection and waging War against us. He has plundered our seas, ravaged our Coasts, burnt our towns, and destroyed the lives of our people. He is at this time transporting large Armies of foreign Mercenaries to compleat the works of death, desolation and tyranny, already begun with circumstances of Cruelty & perfidy scarcely paralleled in the most barbarous ages, and totally unworthy of the Head of a civilized nation. He has constrained our fellow Citizens taken Captive on the high Seas to bear Arms against their Country, to become the executioners of their friends and Brethren, or to fall themselves by their hands. He has excited domestic insurrections amongst us, and has endeavoured to bring on the inhabitants of our frontiers, the merciless Indian Savages, whose known rule of warfare, is an undistinguished destruction of all ages, sexes and conditions. In every stage of these Oppressions We have Petitioned for Redress in the most humble terms: Our repeated Petitions have been answered only by repeated injury. A Prince whose character is thus marked by every act which may define a Tyrant, is unfit to be the ruler of a free people. Nor have We been wanting in attentions to our British brethren. We have warned them from time to time of attempts by their legislature to extend an unwarrantable jurisdiction over us; We have reminded them of the circumstances of our emigration and settlement here. We have appealed to their native justice and magnanimity, and we have conjured them by the ties of our common kindred to disavow these usurpations, which would inevitably interrupt our connections and correspondence. They too have been deaf to the voice of justice and of consanguinity. We must, therefore, acquiesce in the necessity, which denounces our Separation, and hold them, as we hold the rest of mankind, Enemies in War, in Peace Friends.

We, therefore, the Representatives of the united States of America, in General Congress, Assembled, appealing to the Supreme Judge of the world for the rectitude of our intentions do, in the Name, and by the Authority of the good People of these Colonies, solemnly publish and declare, That these United Colonies are, and of Right ought to be Free and Independent States; that they are Absolved from all Allegiance to the British Crown, and that all political connection between them and the State of Great Britain, is and ought to be totally dissolved; and that as Free and Independent States, they have full Power to levy War, conclude Peace, contract Alliances, establish Commerce, and to do all other Acts and things which Independent States may of right do. And for the support of this Declaration, with a firm reliance on the protection of divine Providence, we mutually pledge to each other our lives, our Fortunes and our sacred Honor.

The Declaration of the Rights of Man and Citizen

Originally drafted by a committee of five, this historic document was approved by the French National Assembly in August of 1789. It later served as preamble to the 1791 Constitution, which allowed Louis XVI to continue ruling as a constitutional monarch.

Some have argued that Thomas Jefferson, who was then American ambassador at the French court, influenced the wording of the draft document. In any case, the Declaration of the Rights of Man and the American Declaration of Independence both embodied the universalistic themes of the Age of Enlightenment, the ideas of Montesquieu, Rousseau, and Voltaire.

The representatives of the French people, constituted in National Assembly, considering that the ignorance, neglect, and contempt of the Rights of Man, are the sole causes of public misfortunes and the corruption of governments, have resolved to expose, in solemn Declaration, the natural, inalienable, and sacred Rights of Man, in order that this Declaration, constantly remind them of their rights and duties; in order that the acts of the legislative power and those of the executive power, liable at any moment to be compared with the aims of all political institutions, may be the more respected; in order that the appeals of citizens, founded henceforth on simple and incontestable principles, may always tend to maintain the Constitution and the happiness of all men.

In consequence, the National Assembly recognizes and declares, in the presence and under the auspices of the Supreme Being, the following Rights of Man and of the Citizen:

1. Men are born, and remain, free and equal before the law. Social distinctions can be founded only on public utility.

2. The aim of all political associations is the conservation of the natural and imprescriptible rights of man. These rights are liberty, property, security, and resistance to oppression.

3. The principle of all sovereignty resides in the Nation. No body, no individual, can exercise authority which does not emanate expressly therefrom.

4.   Liberty consists in being able to do whatever does not injure another. Thus the exercise of every man's natural rights is limited only by those which assure the other members of society of these same rights. These limits can be determined only by law.

5.   The law has the right to prohibit only those actions which are harmful to society. All that is not prohibited by law cannot be hindered; and no one can be compelled to do what the law does not require.

6.   The law is the expression of the general will. All citizens have the right to take part in person or through their representatives in its formulation. It must be the same for all, whether it protects or whether it punishes. All citizens being equal in the eyes of the law are equally eligible to all honors, offices, and public employments, according to their abilities and without other distinction than that of their virtues and talents.

7.   No man can be accused, arrested, or detained except in cases determined by the law and according to the forms prescribed thereby. Those who solicit, promote, execute, or cause to be executed arbitrary orders shall be punished; but a citizen summoned or seized by virtue of the law must obey immediately: he becomes guilty if he resists.

8.   The law must establish only those penalties which are strictly and evidently necessary; and no person can be punished except by virtue of law that has been established and promulgated before the offense, and is legally applied.

9.   Since every man is presumed to be innocent until he has been pronounced guilty, if it is judged indispensable to arrest him, all rigorous measures not necessary to secure his person ought to be severely repressed by law.

10.   No man is to be molested on account of his opinions, even his religious opinions, provided that their manifestation does not disturb the public order established by law.

11.   The free communication of thoughts and opinions is one of man's most precious rights. Every citizen may therefore speak, write, and publish freely; except that he shall be responsible for the abuse of that freedom in cases determined by law.

12.   The guarantee of the Rights of Man and of the Citizen makes necessary a public force. This force is therefore instituted for the advantage of all, and not for the particular use of those to whom it is confided.

13.   For the maintenance of public force and the expenses of administration, a common contribution is indispensable. It must be equally apportioned among all citizens according to their abilities.

14.   All citizens have the right to determine, themselves or through their representatives, the necessity of public contributions; to consent to them freely; to watch over the use thereof; and to fix their amount, assessment, collection, and duration.

15. Society has the right to ask an accounting from all public agents of their administration.

16. Any society in which the guarantee of Rights is not assured, nor the separation of Powers determined, has no Constitution.

17. Since property is an inviolable and sacred right, no man may be deprived of it except when public necessity, lawfully constituted, evidently requires it; and on condition that a just indemnity be paid in advance.

The Declaration of the Rights of Woman

September 1791

Olympe de Gouges

Marie Gouze (1748–1793) was a self-educated butcher's daughter from the south of France who, under the name Olympe de Gouges, wrote pamphlets and plays on a variety of issues, including slavery, which she attacked as based on greed and blind prejudice. In this pamphlet she provides a declaration of the rights of women to parallel the one for men, thus criticizing the deputies for having forgotten women. She addressed the pamphlet to the queen, Marie Antoinette, although she also warned the queen that she must work for the Revolution or risk destroying the monarchy altogether. In her postscript she denounced the customary treatment of women as objects easily abandoned. She appended to the declaration a sample form for a marriage contract that called for communal sharing of property. De Gouges went to the guillotine in 1793, condemned as a counterrevolutionary and denounced as an "unnatural" woman.

To be decreed by the National Assembly in its last session or by the next legislature.

Preamble

Mothers, daughters, sisters, female representatives of the nation ask to be constituted as a national assembly. Considering that ignorance, neglect, or contempt for the rights of woman are the sole causes of public misfortunes and governmental corruption, they have resolved to set forth in a solemn declaration the natural, inalienable, and sacred rights of woman: so that by being constantly present to all the members of the social body this declaration may always remind them of their rights and duties; so that by being liable at every moment to comparison with the aim of any and all political institutions the acts of women's and men's powers may be the more fully respected; and so that by being founded henceforward on simple and incontestable principles the demands of the citizenesses may always tend toward maintaining the constitution, good morals, and the general welfare.

In consequence, the sex that is superior in beauty as in courage, needed in maternal sufferings, recognizes and declares, in the presence and under the auspices of the Supreme Being, the following rights of woman and the citizeness.

1. Woman is born free and remains equal to man in rights. Social distinctions may be based only on common utility.

2. The purpose of all political association is the preservation of the natural and imprescriptible rights of woman and man. These rights are liberty, property, security, and especially resistance to oppression.

3. The principle of all sovereignty rests essentially in the nation, which is but the reuniting of woman and man. No body and no individual may exercise authority which does not emanate expressly from the nation.

4. Liberty and justice consist in restoring all that belongs to another; hence the exercise of the natural rights of woman has no other limits than those that the perpetual tyranny of man opposes to them; these limits must be reformed according to the laws of nature and reason.

5. The laws of nature and reason prohibit all actions which are injurious to society. No hindrance should be put in the way of anything not prohibited by these wise and divine laws, nor may anyone be forced to do what they do not require.

6. The law should be the expression of the general will. All citizenesses and citizens should take part, in person or by their representatives, in its formation. It must be the same for everyone. All citizenesses and citizens, being equal in its eyes, should be equally admissible to all public dignities, offices, and employments, according to their ability, and with no other distinction than that of their virtues and talents.

7. No woman is exempted; she is indicted, arrested, and detained in the cases determined by the law. Women like men obey this rigorous law.

8. Only strictly and obviously necessary punishments should be established by the law, and no one may be punished except by virtue of a law established and promulgated before the time of the offense, and legally applied to women.

9. Any woman being declared guilty, all rigor is exercised by the law.

10. No one should be disturbed for his fundamental opinions; woman has the right to mount the scaffold, so she should have the right equally to mount the tribune, provided that these manifestations do not trouble public order as established by law.

11. The free communication of thoughts and opinions is one of the most precious of the rights of woman, since this liberty assures the recognition of children by their fathers. Every citizeness may therefore say freely, I am the mother of your child; a barbarous prejudice [against unmarried women having children] should not force her to hide the

truth, so long as responsibility is accepted for any abuse of this liberty in cases determined by the law [women are not allowed to lie about the paternity of their children].

12. The safeguard of the rights of woman and citizeness requires public powers. These powers are instituted for the advantage of all and not for the private benefit of those to whom they are entrusted.

13. For maintenance of public authority and for expenses of administration, taxation of women and men is equal; she takes part in all forced labor service, in all painful tasks; she must therefore have the same proportion in the distribution of places, employments, offices, dignities, and in industry.

14. The citizenesses and citizens have the right, by themselves or through their representatives, to have demonstrated to them the necessity of public taxes. The citizenesses can only agree to them upon admission of an equal division, not only in wealth, but also in the public administration, and to determine the means of apportionment, assessment, and collection, and the duration of the taxes.

15. The mass of women, joining with men in paying taxes, have the right to hold accountable every public agent of the administration.

16. Any society in which the guarantee of rights is not assured or the separation of powers not settled has no constitution. The constitution is null and void if the majority of individuals composing the nation has not cooperated in its drafting.

17. Property belongs to both sexes whether united or separated; it is for each of them an inviolable and sacred right, and no one may be deprived of it as a true patrimony of nature, except when public necessity, certified by law, obviously requires it, and then on condition of a just compensation in advance.

Postscript

Women, wake up; the tocsin of reason sounds throughout the universe; recognize your rights. The powerful empire of nature is no longer surrounded by prejudice, fanaticism, superstition, and lies. The torch of truth has dispersed all the clouds of folly and usurpation. Enslaved man has multiplied his force and needs yours to break his chains. Having become free, he has become unjust toward his companion. Oh women! Women, when will you cease to be blind? What advantages have you gathered in the revolution? A scorn more marked, a disdain more conspicuous. During the centuries of corruption you only reigned over the weakness of men. Your empire is destroyed; what is left to you then? Firm belief in the injustices of men. The reclaiming of your patrimony founded on the wise decrees of nature; why should you fear such a beautiful enterprise? . . . Whatever the barriers set up against you, it is in your power to overcome them; you only have to want it. Let us pass now to the appalling account of what you have been in society; and since national education is an issue at this moment, let us see if our wise legislators will think sanely about the education of women.

Women have done more harm than good. Constraint and dissimulation have been their lot. What force has taken from them, ruse returned to them; they have had recourse to all the resources of their charms, and the most irreproachable man has not resisted them. Poison, the sword, women controlled everything; they ordered up crimes as much as virtues. For centuries, the French government, especially, depended on the nocturnal administration of women; officials kept no secrets from their indiscretion; ambassadorial posts, military commands, the ministry, the presidency [of a court], the papacy, the college of cardinals, in short everything that characterizes the folly of men, profane and sacred, has been submitted to the cupidity and ambition of this sex formerly considered despicable and respected, and since the revolution, respectable and despised. . . .

Under the former regime, everyone was vicious, everyone guilty. . . . A woman only had to be beautiful and amiable; when she possessed these two advantages, she saw a hundred fortunes at her feet. . . . The most indecent woman could make herself respectable with gold; the commerce in women was a kind of industry amongst the highest classes, which henceforth will enjoy no more credit. If it still did, the revolution would be lost, and in the new situation we would still be corrupted. Can reason hide the fact that every other road to fortune is closed to a woman bought by a man, bought like a slave from the coasts of Africa? The difference between them is great; this is known. The slave [that is, the woman] commands her master, but if the master gives her her freedom without compensation and at an age when the slave has lost all her charms, what does this unfortunate woman become? The plaything of disdain; even the doors of charity are closed to her; she is poor and old, they say; why did she not know how to make her fortune?

Other examples even more touching can be provided to reason. A young woman without experience, seduced by the man she loves, abandons her parents to follow him; the ingrate leaves her after a few years and the older she will have grown with him, the more his inconstancy will be inhuman. If she has children, he will still abandon her. If he is rich, he will believe himself excused from sharing his fortune with his noble victims. If some engagement ties him to his duties, he will violate it while counting on support from the law. If he is married, every other obligation loses its force. What laws then remain to be passed that would eradicate vice down to its roots? That of equally dividing [family] fortunes between men and women and of public administration of their goods. It is easy to imagine that a woman born of a rich family would gain much from the equal division of property [between children]. But what about the woman born in a poor family with merit and virtues; what is her lot? Poverty and opprobrium. If she does not excel in music or painting, she cannot be admitted to any public function, even if she is fully qualified. . . .

Marriage is the tomb of confidence and love. A married woman can give bastards to her husband with impunity, and even the family fortune which does not belong to them. An unmarried woman has only a feeble right: ancient and inhuman laws refuse her the right to the name and goods of her children's father; no new laws have been made in this matter. If giving my sex an honorable and just consistency is considered to be at this time paradoxical on my part and an attempt at the impossible, I leave to future men the glory of dealing with this matter; but while waiting, we can prepare the way with national education, with the restoration of morals and with conjugal agreements.

Form for a Social Contract Between Man and Woman

We, _____ and _____, moved by our own will, unite for the length of our lives and for the duration of our mutual inclinations under the following conditions: We intend and wish to make our wealth communal property, while reserving the right to divide it in favor of our children and of those for whom we might have a special inclination, mutually recognizing that our goods belong directly to our children, from whatever bed they come [legitimate or not], and that all of them without distinction have the right to bear the name of the fathers and mothers who have acknowledged them, and we impose on ourselves the obligation of subscribing to the law that punishes any rejection of one's own blood [refusing to acknowledge an illegitimate child]. We likewise obligate ourselves, in the case of a separation, to divide our fortune equally and to set aside the portion the law designates for our children. In the case of a perfect union, the one who dies first will give up half his property in favor of the children; and if there are no children, the survivor will inherit by right, unless the dying person has disposed of his half of the common property in favor of someone he judges appropriate. [She then goes on to defend her contract against the inevitable objections of "hypocrites, prudes, the clergy, and all the hellish gang."]

Justification of the Use of Terror

Maximilien Robespierre

Maximilien Robespierre (1758–1794) was the leader of the twelve–man Committee of Public Safety elected by the National Convention, which effectively governed France at the height of the radical phase of the revolution. He had once been a fairly straightforward liberal thinker—reputedly he slept with a copy of Rousseau's Social Contract at his side. But his own purity of belief led him to impatience with others.

The committee was among the most creative executive bodies ever seen—and rapidly put into effect policies which stabilized the French economy and began the formation of the very successful French army. It also directed its energies against counter-revolutionary uprisings, especially in the south and west of France. In doing so it unleashed the reign of terror. Here Robespierre, in his speech of February 5, 1794, from which excerpts are given here, discussed this issue. The figures behind this speech indicate that in the five months from September, 1793, to February 5, 1794, the revolutionary tribunal in Paris convicted and executed 238 men and 31 women and acquitted 190 persons, and that on February 5 there were 5,434 individuals in the prisons in Paris awaiting trial.

Robespierre was frustrated with the progress of the revolution. After issuing threats to the National Convention, he himself was arrested in July 1794. He tried to shoot himself but missed, and spent his last few hours with his jaw hanging off. He was guillotined, as a victim of the terror, on July 28, 1794.

But, to found and consolidate democracy, to achieve the peaceable reign of the constitutional laws, we must end the war of liberty against tyranny and pass safely across the storms of the revolution: such is the aim of the revolutionary system that you have enacted. Your conduct, then, ought also to be regulated by the stormy circumstances in which the republic is placed; and the plan of your administration must result from the spirit of the revolutionary government combined with the general principles of democracy.

Now, what is the fundamental principle of the democratic or popular government—that is, the essential spring which makes it move? It is virtue; I am speaking of the public virtue which effected so many prodigies in Greece and Rome and which ought to produce much more surprising ones in republican France; of that virtue which is nothing other than the love of country and of its laws.

But as the essence of the republic or of democracy is equality, it follows that the love of country necessarily includes the love of equality.

It is also true that this sublime sentiment assumes a preference for the public interest over every particular interest; hence the love of country presupposes or produces all the virtues: for what are they other than that spiritual strength which renders one capable of those sacrifices? And how could the slave of avarice or ambition, for example, sacrifice his idol to his country?

Not only is virtue the soul of democracy; it can exist only in that government. . . .

Republican virtue can be considered in relation to the people and in relation to the government; it is necessary in both. When only the government lacks virtue, there remains a resource in the people's virtue; but when the people itself is corrupted, liberty is already lost.

Fortunately virtue is natural to the people, notwithstanding aristocratic prejudices. A nation is truly corrupted when, having by degrees lost its character and its liberty, it passes from democracy to aristocracy or to monarchy; that is the decrepitude and death of the body politic. . . .

But when, by prodigious efforts of courage and reason, a people breaks the chains of despotism to make them into trophies of liberty; when by the force of its moral temperament it comes, as it were, out of the arms of the death, to recapture all the vigor of youth; when by turns it is sensitive and proud, intrepid and docile, and can be stopped neither by impregnable ramparts nor by the innumerable armies of the tyrants armed against it, but stops of itself upon confronting the law's image; then if it does not climb rapidly to the summit of its destinies, this can only be the fault of those who govern it.

From all this let us deduce a great truth: the characteristic of popular government is confidence in the people and severity towards itself.

The whole development of our theory would end here if you had only to pilot the vessel of the Republic through calm waters; but the tempest roars, and the revolution imposes on you another task.

This great purity of the French revolution's basis, the very sublimity of its objective, is precisely what causes both our strength and our weakness. Our strength, because it gives to us truth's ascendancy over imposture, and the rights of the public interest over private interests; our weakness, because it rallies all vicious men against us, all those who in their hearts contemplated despoiling the people and all those who intend to let it be despoiled with impunity, both those who have rejected freedom as a personal calamity and those who have embraced the revolution as a career and the Republic as prey. Hence the defection of so many ambitious or greedy men who since the point of departure have abandoned us along the way because they did not begin the journey with the same destination in view. The two opposing spirits that have been represented in a struggle to rule nature might be said to be fighting in this great period of human history to fix irrevocably the world's destinies, and France is the scene of this fearful combat. Without, all the tyrants encircle you; within, all tyranny's friends conspire; they will conspire until hope is wrested from crime. We must smother the internal and external enemies of the Republic or perish with it; now in this situation, the first maxim of your policy ought to be to lead the people by reason and the people's enemies by terror.

If the spring of popular government in time of peace is virtue, the springs of popular government in revolution are at once *virtue and terror:* virtue, without which terror is fatal; terror, without which virtue is powerless. Terror is nothing other than justice, prompt, severe, inflexible; it is therefore an emanation of virtue; it is not so much a special principle as it is a consequence of the general principle of democracy applied to our country's most urgent needs.

It has been said that terror is the principle of despotic government. Does your government therefore resemble despotism? Yes, as the sword that gleams in the hands of the heroes of liberty resembles that with which the henchmen of tyranny are armed. Let the despot govern by terror his brutalized subjects; he is right, as a despot. Subdue by terror the enemies of liberty, and you will be right, as founders of the Republic. The government of the revolution is liberty's despotism against tyranny. Is force made only to protect crime? And is the thunderbolt not destined to strike the heads of the proud?

. . . Indulgence for the royalists, cry certain men, mercy for the villains! No! mercy for the innocent, mercy for the weak, mercy for the unfortunate, mercy for humanity.

Society owes protection only to peaceable citizens; the only citizens in the Republic are the republicans. For it, the royalists, the conspirators are only strangers or, rather, enemies. This terrible war waged by liberty against tyranny—is it not indivisible? Are the enemies within not the allies of the enemies without? The assassins who tear our country apart, the intriguers who buy the consciences that hold the people's mandate; the traitors who sell them; the mercenary pamphleteers hired to dishonor the people's cause, to kill public virtue, to stir up the fire of civil discord, and to prepare political counterrevolution by moral counterrevolution—are all those men less guilty or less dangerous than the tyrants whom they serve?

The World We Have Lost

Peter Laslett

The following has been excerpted from the 1965 book The World We Have Lost. *Laslett (1915–2001) was a cultural and intellectual historian at Cambridge University, whose work exploded numerous misperceptions about early modern English society.*

In the year 1619 the bakers of London applied to the authorities for an increase in the price of bread. They sent in support of their claims a complete description of a bakery and an account of its weekly costs. There were thirteen or fourteen people in such an establishment: the baker and his wife, four paid employees who were called journeymen, two apprentices, two maid-servants and the three or four children of the master baker himself. Six pounds ten shillings a week was reckoned to be the outgoings of this establishment of which only eleven shillings and eight-pence went for wages: half a crown a week for each of the journeymen and ten-pence for each of the maids. Far and away the greatest cost was for food: two pounds nine shillings out of the six pounds ten shillings, at five shillings a head for the baker and his wife, four shillings a head for their helpers and two shillings for their children. It cost much more in food to keep a journeyman than it cost in money; four times as much to keep a maid. Clothing was charged up too, not only for the man, wife and children, but for the apprentices as well. Even school fees were claimed as a justifiable charge on the price of bread for sale, and it cost sixpence a week for the teaching and clothing of a baker's child.

A London bakery was undoubtedly what we should call a commercial or even an industrial undertaking, turning out loaves by the thousand. Yet the business was carried on in the house of the baker himself. There was probably a *shop* as part of the house, *shop* as in work*shop* and not as meaning a retail establishment. Loaves were not ordinarily sold over the counter: they had to be carried to the open-air market and displayed on stalls. There was a garner behind the house, for which the baker paid two shillings a week in rent, and where he kept his wheat, his *seacoal* for the fire and his store of salt. The house itself was one of those high, half-timbered overhanging structures on the narrow London street which we always think of when we remember the scene in which Shakespeare, Pepys or even Christopher Wren lived. Most of it was taken up with the living-quarters of the dozen people who worked there.

It is obvious that all these people ate in the house since the cost of their food helped to determine the production cost of the bread. Except for the journeymen they were all obliged to sleep in the house at night and live together as a family.

The only word used at that time to describe such a group of people was "family." The man at the head of the group, the entrepreneur, the employer, or the manager, was then known as the master or head of the family. He was father to some of its members and in place of father to the rest. There was no sharp distinction between his domestic and his economic functions. His wife was both his partner and his subordinate, a partner because she ran the family, took charge of the food and managed the women-servants, a subordinate because she was woman and wife, mother and in place of mother to the rest.

The paid servants of both sexes had their specified and familiar position in the family, as much part of it as the children but not quite in the same position. At that time the family was not one society only but three societies fused together: the society of man and wife, of parents and children and of master and servant. But when they were young, and servants were, for the most part, young, unmarried people, they were very close to children in their status and their function. Here is the agreement made between the parents of a boy about to become an apprentice and his future master. The boy covenants to dwell as an apprentice with his master for seven years, to keep his secrets and to obey his commandments.

> Taverns and alehouses he shall not haunt, dice, cards or any other unlawful games he shall not use, fornication with any woman he shall not commit, matrimony with any woman he shall not contract. He shall not absent himself by night or by day without his master's leave but be a true and faithful servant.

On his side, the master undertakes to teach his apprentice his art, science or occupation with moderate correction.

> Finding and allowing unto his said servant meat, drink, apparel, washing, lodging and all other things during the said term of seven years, and to give unto his said apprentice at the end of the said term double apparel, to wit, one suit for holydays and one suit for worken days.

Apprentices, therefore, were workers who were also children, extra sons or extra daughters (for girls could be apprenticed too), clothed and educated as well as fed, obliged to obedience and forbidden to marry, unpaid and absolutely dependent until the age of twenty-one. If apprentices were workers in the position of sons and daughters, the sons and daughters of the house were workers too. John Locke laid it down in 1697 that the children of the poor must work for some part of the day when they reached the age of three. The sons and daughters of a London baker were not free to go to school for many years of their young lives, or even to play as they wished when they came back home. Soon they would find themselves doing what they could in *bolting*, that is sieving flour, or in helping the maidservant with her panniers of loaves on the way to the market stall, or in playing their small parts in preparing the never-ending succession of meals for the whole household.

We may see at once, therefore, that the world we have lost, as I have chosen to call it, was no paradise or golden age of equality, tolerance or loving kindness.

It is so important that I should not be misunderstood on this point that I will say at once that the coming of industry cannot be shown to have brought economic oppression and exploitation along with it. It was there already. The patriarchal arrangements which we have begun to explore were not new in the England of Shakespeare and Elizabeth. They were as old as the Greeks, as old as European history, and not confined to Europe. And it may well be that they abused and enslaved people quite as remorselessly as the economic arrangements which had replaced them in the England of Blake and Victoria. When people could expect to live for only thirty years in all, how must a man have felt when he realized that so much of his adult life, perhaps all, must go in working for his keep and very little more in someone else's family?

But people do not recognize facts of this sort, and no one is content to expect to live as long as the majority in fact will live. Every servant in the old social world was probably quite confident that he or she would some day get married and be at the head of a new family, keeping others in subordination. If it is legitimate to use the words exploitation and oppression in thinking of the economic arrangements of the pre-industrial world, there are nevertheless differences in the manner of oppressing and exploiting. The ancient order of society was felt to be eternal and unchangeable by those who supported, enjoyed and endured it. There was no expectation of reform. How could there be when economic organization was domestic organization, and relationships were rigidly regulated by the social system, by the content of Christianity itself?

Here is a vivid contrast with social expectation in Victorian England, or in industrial countries everywhere today. Every relationship in our world which can be seen to affect our economic life is open to change, is expected indeed to change of itself, or if it does not, to *be* changed, made better, by an omnicompetent authority. This makes for a less stable social world, though it is only one of the features of our society which impels us all in that direction. All industrial societies, we may suppose, are far less stable than their predecessors. They lack the extraordinarily cohesive influence which familial relationships carry with them, that power of reconciling the frustrated and the discontented by emotional means. Social revolution, meaning an irreversible changing of the pattern of social relationships, never happened in traditional, patriarchal, pre-industrial human society. It was almost impossible to contemplate.

Almost, but not quite. Sir Thomas More, in the reign of Henry VIII, could follow Plato in imagining a life where children would not know their parents and where promiscuity could be a political institution. Sir William Petty, 150 years later, one of the very first of the political sociologists, could speculate about polygamy; and the England of the Tudors and the Stuarts already knew of social structures and sexual arrangements, existing in the newly discovered world, which were alarmingly different from their own. But it must have been an impossible effort of the imagination to suppose that they were anything like as satisfactory.

It will be noticed that the roles we have allotted to all the members of the capacious family of the master-baker of London in the year 1619 are, emotionally, all highly symbolic and highly satisfactory. We may feel that in a whole society organized like this, in spite of all the subordination, the exploitation and the obliteration of those who were young, or feminine, or in service, everyone belonged in a group, a family group. Everyone had his circle of affection: every relationship could be seen as a love-relationship.

Not so with us. Who could love the name of a limited company or of a government department as an apprentice could love his superbly satisfactory father-figure master, even if he were a bully and a beater, a usurer and a hypocrite? But if a family is a circle of affection, it can also be the scene of hatred. The worst tyrants among human beings, the murderers and the villains, are jealous husbands and resentful wives, possessive partners and deprived children. In the traditional, patriarchal society of Europe, where practically everyone lived out his whole life within the family, often within one family only, tension like this must have been incessant and unrelieved, incapable of release except in crisis. Men, women and children have to be very close together for a very long time to generate the emotional power which can give rise to a tragedy of Sophocles, or Shakespeare, or Racine. Conflict in such a society was between individual people, on the personal scale. Except when the Christians fought with the infidels, or Protestants fought with Catholics, clashes between masses of persons did not often arise. There could never be a situation such as that which makes our own time, as some men say, the scene of perpetual revolution.

All this is true to history only if the little knot of people making bread in Stuart London was indeed the typical social unit of the old world in its size, composition and scale. There are reasons why a baker's household might have been a little out of the ordinary, for baking was a highly traditional occupation in a society increasingly subject to economic change. We shall see, in due course, that a family of thirteen people, which was also a unit of production of thirteen, less the children quite incapable of work, was quite large for English society at that time. Only the families of the really important, the nobility and the gentry, the aldermen and the successful merchants, were ordinarily as large as this. In fact, we can take the bakery to represent the upper limit in size and scale of the group in which ordinary people lived and worked. Among the great mass of society which cultivated the land, and which will be the major preoccupation of this essay, the family group was smaller than a London craftsman's entourage. . . . One reason for feeling puzzled by our own industrial society is that the historian has never set out to tell us what society was like before industry came and seems to assume that everyone knows.

We shall have much more to say about the movement of servants from farmhouse to farmhouse in the old world, and shall return to the problem of understanding ourselves in time, in contrast with our ancestors. Let us emphasize again the scale of life in the working family of the London baker. Few persons in the old world ever found themselves in groups larger than family groups, and there were few families of more than a dozen members. The largest household so far known to us, apart from the royal court and the establishments of the nobility, lay and spiritual, is that of Sir Richard Newdigate, Baronet, in his house of Arbury, within his parish of Chilvers Coton in Warwickshire, in the year 1684. There were thirty-seven people in Sir Richard's family: himself; Lady Mary Newdigate his wife; seven daughters, all under the age of sixteen; and twenty-eight servants, seventeen men and boys and eleven women and girls. This was still a family, not an institution, a staff, an office or a firm.

Everything physical was on the human scale, for the commercial worker in London, and the miner who lived and toiled in Newdigate's village of Chilvers Coton. No object in England was larger than London Bridge or St. Paul's Cathedral, no structure in the Western World to stand comparison with the Colosseum in Rome.

Everything temporal was tied to the human life-span, too. The death of the master baker, head of the family, ordinarily meant the end of the bakery. Of course there might be a son to succeed, but the master's surviving children would be young if he himself had lived only as long as most men. Or an apprentice might fulfill the final function of apprenticehood, substitute sonship, that is to say, and marry his master's daughter, or even his widow. Surprisingly often, the widow, if she could, would herself carry on the trade. . . .

We may pause here to point out that our argument is not complete. There was an organization in the social structure of Europe before the coming of industry which enormously exceeded the family in size and endurance. This was the Christian church. It is true to say that the ordinary person, especially the female, never went to a gathering larger than could assemble in an ordinary house except when going to church. When we look at the aristocracy and the church from the point of view of the scale of life and the impermanence of all man-made institutions, we can see that their functions were such as make very little sense in an industrial society like our own. Complicated arrangements then existed, and still exist in England now, which were intended to make it easier for the noble family to give the impression that it had indeed always persisted. Such, for example, were those intricate rules of succession which permitted a cousin, however distant, to succeed to the title and to the headship, provided only he was in the male line. Such was the final remedy in the power of the Crown, the fountain of honour, to declare that an anomalous succession should take place. Nobility was forever.

But the symbolic provision of permanence is only the beginning of the social functions of the church. At a time when the ability to read with understanding and to write much more than a personal letter was confined for the most part to the ruling minority, in a society which was otherwise oral in its communications, the preaching parson was the great link between the illiterate mass and the political, technical and educated world. Sitting in the 10,000 parish churches of England every Sunday morning, in groups of 20, 50, 100 or 200, the illiterate mass of the people were not only taking part in the single group activity which they ordinarily shared with others outside their own families. They were informing themselves in the only way open to them of what went on in England, Europe, and the world as a whole. The priesthood was indispensable to the religious activity of the old world, at a time when religion was still of primary interest and importance. But the priesthood was also indispensable because of its functions in social communication.

Not only did the scale of their work and the size of the group which was engaged make them exceptional, the constitution of the group did too. In the baking household we have chosen as our standard, sex and age were mingled together. Fortunate children might go out to school, but adults did not usually go out to work. There was nothing to correspond to the thousands of young men on the assembly line, the hundreds of young women in the offices, the lonely lives of housekeeping wives which we now know only too well. We shall see that those who survived to old age in the much less favourable conditions for survival which then were prevalent, were surprisingly often left to live and die alone, in their tiny cottages or sometimes in the almshouses which were being built so widely in the England of the Tudors and the Stuarts. Poor-law establishments, parochial in purpose and in size, had begun their melancholy chapter in the history of the English people. But institutional life was otherwise almost unknown. There were no hotels, hostels, or blocks of flats for single persons, very few hospitals and none of the kind we are familiar with, almost no young men and women living on their own. The family group where so great a majority lived was what we should undoubtedly call a "balanced" and "healthy" group.

When we turn from the hand-made city of London to the hand-moulded immensity of rural England, we may carry the same sentimental prejudice along with us. To every farm there was a family, which spread itself over its portion of the village lands as the family of the master-craftsman filled out his manufactory. When a holding was small, and most were small as are the tiny holdings of European peasants today, a man tilled it with the help of his wife and his children. No single man, we must remember, would usually take charge of the land, any more than a single man would often be found at the head of a workshop in the city. The master of a family was expected to be a householder, whether he was a butcher, a baker, a candlestick maker or simply a husbandman, which was the universal name for one whose skill was in working the land. Marriage we must insist, and it is one of the rules which gave its character to the society of our ancestors, was the entry to full membership, in the enfolding countryside, as well as in the scattered urban centres.

But there was a difference in scale and organization of work on the land and in the town. The necessities of rural life did require recurrent groupings of households for common economic purposes, occasionally something like a crowd of men, women and children working together for days on end. Where the ground was still being tilled as open fields, and each household had a number of strips scattered all over the whole open area and not a compact collection of enclosures, ploughing was cooperative, as were many other operations, above all harvesting, and this continued even after enclosure. We do not yet know how important this element of enforced common activity was in the life of the English rural community on the eve of industrialization, or how much difference enclosure made in this respect. But whatever the situation was, the economic transformation of the eighteenth and nineteenth centuries destroyed communality altogether in English rural life. The group of men from several farmsteads working the heavy plough in springtime, the bevy of harvesters from every house in the village wading into the high standing grass to begin the cutting of the hay, had no successors in large-scale economic activity. For the arrangement of these groups was entirely different in principle from the arrangement of a factory, or a firm, or even of a collective farm.

Both before and after enclosure, some peasants did well: their crops were heavier and they had more land to till. To provide the extra labour needed then, the farming householder, like the successful craftsman, would extend his working family by taking on young men and women as servants to live with him and work the fields. This he would have to do, even if the land which he was farming was not his own but rented from the great family in the manor house. Sometimes, we have found, he would prefer to send out his own children as servants and bring in other children and young men to do the work. This is one of the few glimpses we can get into the quality of the emotional life of the family at this time, for it shows that parents may have been unwilling to submit children of their own to the discipline of work at home. It meant, too, that servants were not simply the perquisites of wealth and position. A quarter, or a third, of all the families in the country contained servants in Stuart times, and this meant that very humble people had them as well as the titled and the wealthy. Most of the servants, moreover, male or female, in the great house and in the small, were engaged in working the land.

The boys and the men would do the ploughing, hedging, carting and the heavy, skilled work of the harvest. The women and the girls would keep the house, prepare the meals, make the butter and the cheese, the bread and the beer, and would also look after the cattle and take the fruit to market. At harvest-time, from June to October, every hand was occupied and every back was bent. These were the decisive months for the whole population in our damp northern climate, with its one harvest in a season and reliance on one or two standard crops. So critical was the winning of the grain for bread that the first rule of gentility (a gentleman never worked with his hands for his living) might be abrogated. . . .

The factory won its victory by outproducing the working family, taking away the market for the products of hand-labour and cutting prices to the point where the craftsman had either to starve or take a job under factory discipline himself. It was no sudden, complete and final triumph, for the seamstresses were working in the garrets right up to the twentieth century, and the horrors of sweated labour which so alarmed our grandfathers took place amongst the out-workers, not on the factory floor. It was not a transformation which affected only commerce, industry and the town, for the handwork of the cottages disappeared entirely, till, by the year 1920, rural England was an agrarian remnant, an almost lifeless shell. The process was not English alone, at any points in its development, and its effects on the Continent of Europe were in some ways more obviously devastating than ever they were amongst our people. But ours was the society which first ventured into the industrial era, and English men and women were the first who had to try to find a home for themselves in a world where family and household seemed to have no place.

But Marx and the historians who have followed him were surely wrong to call this process by the simple name of the triumph of capitalism, the rise and victory of the bourgeoisie. The presence of capital, we have seen, was the very circumstance which made it possible in earlier times for the working family to preserve its independence both on the land and in the cities, linking together the scattered households of the workers in such a way that no one had to make the daily double journey from home to workshop, from suburb to office and factory. Capitalism, however defined, did not begin at the time when the working household was endangered by the beginnings of the factory system, and economic inequality was not the product of the social transformation which so quickly followed after. Though the enormous, insolent wealth of the new commercial and industrial fortunes emphasized the iniquity of the division between rich and poor, it is doubtful whether Victorian England was any worse in this respect than the England of the Tudors and the Stuarts. It was not the fact of capitalism alone, not simply the concentration of the means of production in the hands of the few and the reduction of the rest to a position of dependence which opened wide the social gulf, though the writers of the eighteenth and nineteenth centuries give us ample evidence that this was observed and was resented—by the dispossessed peasantry in England especially. More important, it is suggested, far more likely a source for the feeling that there is a world which once we all possessed, a world now passed away, is the fact of the transformation of the family life of everyone which industrialism brought with it.

In the vague and difficult verbiage of our own generation, we can say that the removal of the economic functions from the patriarchal family at the point of industrialization created a mass society. It turned the people who worked into a mass of undifferentiated equals, working in a factory or scattered between the factories and mines, bereft forever of the feeling that work, a family affair, carried with it. The Marxist historical sociology presents this as the growth of class consciousness amongst the proletariat, and this is an important historical truth. But because it belongs with the large-scale class model for all social change it can also be misleading, as we shall hope to show. Moreover it has tended to divert attention from the structural function of the family in the preindustrial world, and made impossible up till now a proper, informed contrast between our world and the lost world we have to analyze. . . .

European society is of the patriarchal type, and with some variations, of which the feudal went the furthest, it remained patriarchal in its institutions right up to the coming of the factories, the offices and the rest. European patriarchalism, we may notice, was of a rather surprising kind, for it was marked by the independence of the nuclear family, man, wife and children, not by the extended family of relatives living together in a group of several generations under the same patriarchal head. Yet society was patriarchal, nevertheless, right up to the time of industrial transformation: it can now no longer be said to be patriarchal at all, except vestigially and in its emotional predisposition. The time has now come to divide our European past in a simpler way with industrialization as the point of critical change.

The word alienation is part of the cant of the mid-twentieth century and it began as an attempt to describe the separation of the worker from his world of work. We need not accept all that this expression has come to convey in order to recognize that it does point to something vital to us all in relation to our past. Time was when the whole of life went forward in the family, in a circle of loved, familiar faces, known and fondled objects, all to human size. That time has gone forever. It makes us very different from our ancestors. . . .

In every one of the village communities too, the families of craftsmen, labourers and paupers tended to be smaller than the families of yeomen, and those of the gentry to be largest. The traffic in children from the humbler to the more successful families shows up in the relative numbers in the various groups. Poverty, in our day, or, at least, in the very recent past, was associated with large numbers of children, but . . . in the seventeenth century exactly the reverse was true. The richer you were, the more children you had in your household. In [the village of Goodnestone] in 1676, the gentry with children had an average of 3.5 in their families, the yeomen 2.9, the tradesmen 2.3, the labourers 2.1 and the paupers 1.8.

These figures from Goodnestone are too good to be true and it is common enough to find humble families with many children at home, too many for the meager resources of the wage-earner and a promise of destitution for his widow if he should die too soon. Nevertheless, the association of few children with modest position and resources is almost as marked a feature of social structure in the traditional world as the association of smaller families generally with the poor. It was not simply a matter of the poor offering up their children to the rich as servants; they probably also had fewer children born to them, and of those which were born, fewer survived. It is likely that works on the expectation of life and size of the biological family will confirm what early impressions seem to show, which is that poor men and their wives could not expect to live together long enough to have as many offspring as the rich. This loss of potential labour-power was a matter of consequence, for it always must be remembered that the actual work on most of the plots of land was done by the working family, the man, his wife and children.

At harvest-time, of course, there was a difference: the individual farming family could no longer cope with the work. From the making of the hay in June until the winning of the corn and pease in late September, every able-bodied person in the village community was at work on everyone's land. How much cooperation there was is difficult to say, but when the crisis of the agricultural year came round, right up to the time of mechanized farming, the village acted as a community. When all was in, there was harvest home.

> It is usual, in most places, after they get all the pease pulled or the last grain down, to invite all the workfolks and their wives (that helped them that harvest) to supper, and then they have puddings, bacon, or boiled beef, flesh or apple pies, and then cream brought in platters, and every one a spoon; then after all they have hot cakes and ale; for they bake cakes and send for ale against that time: some will cut their cake and put it into the cream, and this feast is called cream-pot, or cream-kit; for on the morning that they get all done the workfolks will ask their dames if they have good store of cream and say they must have the cream-kit anon.

This was the Yorkshire custom in the 1640s when it was necessary, at harvest-time, to go even beyond the carpenters, the wheelwrights and the millers, in order to bring in the sheaves off the fields. The richer men had to make a home in the barns during harvest for folk, pastoral in their ways, who came down from the wild moorland. Migration of labour at harvest was common enough in the eighteenth century, but eating and drinking together was a universal characteristic of rural life at all times. Whatever the church-wardens or the overseers of the poor did, when the church-bell was rung in celebration, or the churchyard mowed, there was an entry in the ill-written accounts for ale drunk on the occasion. . . . The meticulous, unpopular Rector of Clayworth in the last quarter of the seventeenth century, entertained the *husbandry* of the two settlements in his parish separately to dinner every year.

When the curate of Goodnestone returned the names of all his parishioners in April, 1676, "according to their families, according to the quality and according to their religion," he did as he was bid and told his lordship, the bishop, how many of them had been to holy communion that Eastertide. Apart from sixteen exceptions every person in the community known by their priest to be qualified for the sacrament had actually taken it at some time during the festival, which fell in that year between March 19th and 26th: 128 people communicated, that is to say, out of a population of 281. Even the defaulters had promised to make amends at Whitsuntide, all but the one family in the village which was nonconformist. But William Wanstall, senior, one of the absentees, was given no such grace; he had been "excluded the

Holy Sacrament for his notorious drunkenness, but since hath promised reformation." Francis Nicholson, the priest-in-charge, was evidently a devoted pastor, for he could give an account of every one of the absentees. Mrs. Elizabeth Richards, the widowed head of one of the households of gentry, was excused as "melancholy," and Barbara Pain since she was "under a dismal calamity, the unnatural death of her husband," who had left her at the head of a yeoman family, three children and two servants.

This . . . draws attention to a feature of the village community and of the whole of the world we have not half-forgotten which has scarcely been mentioned so far. All our ancestors were literal Christian believers, all of the time. Not only zealous priests, such as Francis Nicholson, not only serious-minded laymen, but also the intellectuals and the publicly responsible looked on the Christian religion as the explanation of life, and on religious service as its proper end. Not everyone was equally devout, of course, and it would be simple-minded to suppose that none of these villagers ever had their doubts. Much of their devotion must have been formal, and some of it mere conformity. But their world was a Christian world and their religious activity was spontaneous, not forced on them from above. When Francis Nicholson refused the cup to William Wanstall, in March, 1676, the scores of other people in the church that morning no doubt approved of what he did, as no doubt Wanstall deserved this very public rebuke. When William Sampson, the formidable Rector of Clayworth, did exactly the same thing in April, 1679, to Ralph Meers and Anne Fenton "upon a common fame that they lived and lodged together, not being married," he also had the community behind him. He knew what he was doing too, for Anne Fenton's first baby was christened two months later, only a week or two, presumably, after she had married Ralph Meers.

It has been shown only very recently how it came about that the mass of the English people lost their Christian belief, and how religion came to be a middle-class matter. When the arrival of industry created huge societies of persons in the towns with an entirely different outlook from these Stuart villagers, practically no one went to church, not if he was working class and was left untouched by religious emotion. Christianity was no longer in the social air which everyone breathed together, rich and poor, gentleman, husbandman, artificer, labourer and pauper. So much has been written about the abuses of the clergy, in earlier times, so much about the controversies and doubts, about the revivals, especially the Wesleyan revival, that the religious attitude of common folk has been lost sight of. Perhaps the twelve labourers who lived at Goodnestone in 1767 did not know very clearly what Our Lord's Supper meant, and perhaps they felt that it would displease Squire Hales if they stayed away, but every single one of them took communion. Their descendants in the slums of London in the 1830s, '40s and '50s did not do so: they already looked on Christianity as belonging to the rural world which they had lost. It was something for their employers, something for the respectable, which, perhaps, they might go in for if ever they attained respectability and comfort. This was not true of the hard-working, needy, half-starved labourers of pre-industrial times.

From *The Sadler Report*

Minutes of Evidence
Jovis, 12 die Aprilis, 1832

> *In the early 1830s, the British Parliament commissioned an official study to investigate factory working conditions. The following is an excerpt from the thousands of pages of testimony that were collected and later published as* The Sadler Report. *This investigation ultimately led to some of the first government labor reforms in history, limiting working hours and improving worker safety.*

Michael Thomas Sadler, Esquire in the chair.
William Cooper called in; and Examined.

What is your business?—I follow the cloth-dressing at present.

What is your age?—I was eight-and-twenty last February.

When did you first begin to working in mills or factories?—When I was about 10 years of age.

With whom did you first work?—At Mr. Benyon's flax mills, in Meadow's lane, Leeds.

What were your usual hours of working?—We began at five, and gave over at nine; at five o'clock in the morning.

And you gave over at nine o'clock?—At nine at night.

At what distance might you have lived from the mill?—About a mile and a half.

At what time had you to get up in the morning to attend to your labour?—I had to be up soon after four o'clock.

Every morning?—Every morning.

What intermissions had you for meals?—When we began at five in the morning. We went on until noon, and then we had 40 minutes for dinner.

Had you no time for breakfast?—No, we got it as we could, while we were working.

Had you any time for an afternoon refreshment, or what is called in Yorkshire your "drinking"?—No; when we began at noon, we went till night; there was only one stoppage, the 40 minutes for dinner.

Then as you had to get your breakfast, and what is called "drinking" in that manner, you had to put it on one side?—Yes, we had to put it on one side; and when we got our frames doffed, we ate two or three mouthfuls, and then put it by again.

Is there not considerable dust in a flax mill?—A flax mill is very dusty indeed.

Was not your food therefore frequently spoiled?—Yes, at times with the dust; sometimes we could not eat it, when it had got a lot of dust on.

What were you when you were ten years old?—What is called a bobbin-doffer; when the frames are quite full, we have to doff them.

Then as you lived so far from home, you took your dinner to the mill?—We took all our meals with us, living so far off.

During the 40 minutes which you were allowed for dinner, had you ever to employ that time in your turn in cleaning the machinery?—At times we had to stop to clean the machinery, and then we got our dinner as well as we could; they paid us for that.

At these times you had no resting at all?—No.

How much had you for cleaning the machinery?—I cannot exactly say what they gave us, as I never took any notice of it.

Did you ever work even later than the time you have mentioned?—I cannot say that I worked later there. I had a sister who worked upstairs, and she worked till 11 at night, in what they call the card-room.

At what time in the morning did she begin to work?—At the same time as myself.

And they kept her there till 11 at night?—Till 11 at night.

You say that your sister was in the card-room?—Yes.

Is not that a very dusty department?—Yes, very dusty indeed.

She had to be at the mill at five, and was kept at work till eleven at night?—Yes.

During the whole time she was there?—During the whole time; there was only 40 minutes allowed at dinner out of that.

To keep you at your work for such a length of time, and especially toward the termination of such a day's labour as that, what means were taken to keep you awake and attentive?—They strapped us at times, when we were not quite ready to be doffing the frame when it was full.

Were you frequently strapped?—At times we were frequently strapped.

What sort of strap was it?—About this length [*describing it*].

What was it made of?—Of leather.

Were you occasionally very considerably hurt with the strap?—Sometimes it hurt us very much, and sometimes they did not lay on so hard as they did at others.

Were the girls strapped in that sort of way?—They did not strap what they called the grown-up women.

Were any of the female children strapped?—Yes; they were strapped in the same way as the lesser boys.

What were your wages at 10 years old at Mr. Benyon's?—I think it was 4 *s.* a week.

When you left Mr. Benyon, to what mill did you then go?—To Mr. Clayton's; that was a flax mill.

What age were you when you went there?—I was at Mr. Benyon's nearly a year and a half.

Then you were eleven years and a half old?—Yes.

What were your hours of work at Mr. Clayton's?—We started at five in the morning, and worked till ten minutes past eight at night.

That is 15 hours and 10 minutes?—Yes; and we had only 40 minutes out of that for dinner.

You assembled at five in the morning?—From five in the morning until ten minutes past eight at night.

Had you any time allowed for breakfast or drinking at that mill?—No, it was just the same as the other, with only 40 minutes for dinner.

So that, in point of fact, you had to be attending to your work on your legs for that length of time, with the short intermission of 40 minutes?—Yes, we had to get our meals as we could get them, all out our dinner.

Were your punishments the same in that mill as in the other?—Yes, they used the strap the same there.

How long did you work in that mill?—Five years.

And how did it agree with your health?—I was sometimes well, and sometimes not very well.

Did it affect your breathing at all?—Yes, sometimes we were stuffed.

When your hours were so long, you had not any time to attend to a day-school?—We had no time to go to a day-school, only to a Sunday-school; and then with working such long hours we wanted to have a bit of rest, so that I slept till the afternoon, sometimes till dinner, and sometimes after.

Did you attend a place of worship?—I should have gone to a place of worship many times, but I was in the habit of falling asleep, and that kept me away; I did not like to go for fear of being asleep.

Do you mean that you could not prevent yourself from falling asleep, in consequence of the fatigue of the preceding week?—Yes.

Did you work in any other flax mill?—In no other flax mill.

Did you afterwards work in a woollen mill?—I worked in what they call a cloth-dressing mill.

In whose mill did you next work?—I went to Mr. Pearson's.

What were your hours there?—I think it was from six to eight.

What time was allowed there for meals?—Half an hour for breakfast, an hour at dinner, and half an hour at drinking.

That was 12 hours at the woollen mill?—Yes.

When you left that mill, where did you go to next?—I went to Mr. Wilks's, in Meadow's-lane; that is a cloth mill.

Were your hours the same there?—No; there were short hours there.

Did you find the short hours working suit your health better?—It did a great deal better with me.

Where did you go to then?—To Mr. Giles, in Bowman-lane; that is a cloth mill.

What hours did you work there?—From six to eight, and from six to nine.

With the same intermissions?—Yes, with the same intermissions.

What was the next mill you worked at?—Then I went to Mr. Chorley's.

Were your hours the same there?—Not quite so long there; they were from six to seven.

With the same intervals for meals?—Yes.

You have already stated that your health was better when the labour was shorter?—It was a deal better when only working these hours.

Where did you go then?—To Mr. James Brown's.

What were you at Mr. James Brown's?—I was a gigger and a boiler.

When did you go there?—I should think I must be about 20 years of age when I went there.

Were you a gigger and a boiler when you first went to Mr. Brown's?—I was a gigger when I went to Mr. Brown's; I was a boiler a good while after.

State what was your usual work when you were only a gigger.—When I was only a gigger I went at five o'clock on a Monday morning, and had half an hour at breakfast and an hour at dinner, and half an hour at drinking; then went on till nine on Monday evening, and stopped half an hour; then went on to twelve at midnight, and stopped an hour; then went on to half-past four on Tuesday morning, and stopped half an hour; then went on again from five to eight, and stopped half an hour; then went on till twelve, and stopped an hour; then went on again from one to five, and stopped half an hour; then went on again to nine o'clock at night, when we went home.

What did you do on the Wednesday?—Went again at five o'clock in the morning.

What time did you close at night?—At nine.

What did you do on the Thursday?—Went again on Thursday morning at five, and returned at nine at night. On Friday morning we went at five; worked all Friday, Friday night, and till Saturday evening at five, with the same time for meals as before.

When you became a boiler, will you state the number of hours you had to labour at the same mill?—When I was a boiler, I began work at one o'clock on the Monday morning; went on till five, and stopped half an hour; then went on to eight, and stopped half an hour; then went on to twelve, and stopped an hour; then went on to five, and stopped half an hour; then went on to nine, and stopped half an hour; then went on to twelve, and stopped an hour; then began again, and went on to half-past four on Tuesday morning, and stopped half an hour; then went on to eight, and stopped half an hour; then went on to twelve, and stopped an hour; then went on to five, and stopped half an hour; then went on to nine, and then gave over on the Tuesday night. On Wednesday morning we went at five, and stopped half an hour at breakfast; then went on to twelve, and stopped an hour; then went on to five, and stopped half an hour; then went on to nine, and then gave over. Thursday was the same as Wednesday. On Friday morning we went at five, and stopped half an hour at breakfast; then we went on to twelve, and stopped an hour; then we went on to five, and stopped half an hour; then we went on to nine, and stopped half an hour; then we went on to twelve at midnight, and stopped an hour; then we went on to half-past four, and stopped half an hour; then we went on to eight, and stopped half an hour; then we went on to twelve, and stopped an hour; then we went on to five o'clock on Saturday night, and gave over.

Then in the whole week you had only four nights' rest, exclusive of Sunday night?—No.

And that rest was after nine o'clock, and before five?—Yes.

As I calculate, you laboured as a boiler 44 hours running, from Monday morning till Tuesday night, having 10 intervals, amounting altogether to only six hours and a half; and never going to bed?—You cannot go to bed.

And 36 hours of labour from Friday morning till you were let loose on Saturday evening, including five hours and an half for meals?—Yes.

On Wednesday and Thursday you had, from five till nine, 16 hours of labour, including meals?—Yes.

Then on Monday and Friday nights you had no rest?—No rest.

What was the effect of this excessive labour upon you?—We all felt unwell, and were stiff, and could not make proper use of our limbs till we had worked a little, when it went off.

Had this a serious effect on your health?—Yes, it had a great deal of effect on our health.

But as to yourself personally?—Yes.

After working at a mill to this excess, how did you find your health at last?—I found it very bad indeed; I found illness coming on me a long time before I fell down.

Did you at length become so ill as to be unable to pursue your work?—I was obliged to give it up entirely.

How long were you ill?—For six months.

Who attended?—Mr. Metcalf and Mr. Freeman.

What were you told by your medical attendants was the reason of your illness?—Nothing but hard labour, and working long hours; and they gave me up, and said no good could be done for me, that I must go into the country.

Did this excessive labour not only weaken you but destroy your appetite?—It destroyed the appetite, and I became so feeble that I could not cross the floor unless I had a stick to go with; I was in great pain, and could find ease in no posture.

You could drink in the meantime, if you could not eat?—Yes, I could drink.

But you found that [did] not improve your health?—No.

Has it been remarked that your excessive labour from early life has greatly diminished your growth?—A number of persons have said that such was the case, and that I was the same as if I had been made of iron or stone.

What height are you?—About five feet. It is that that has hindered me of my growth.

When you were somewhat recovered, did you apply for labour?—I applied for my work again, but the overlooker said I was not fit to work; he was sure of that, and he would not let me have it. I was then obliged to throw myself on the parish.

Have you subsisted on the parish ever since?—Yes.

Have you been always willing and anxious to work?—I was always willing and anxious to work from my infancy.

Have you been on the parish since your severe illness?—Yes.

When did you first begin to receive wages yourself?—Ever since I began to work; I gave them to my parents.

How old were you then?—Ten years.

How soon did you begin to work in your own account and make your own bargain with your master for wages?—I always bargained for my wages ever since I began to work for wages; always; my parents never bargained for me. I always bargained for myself.

Not when you were 10 years old?—Yes.

Do you know anything, of your own knowledge, of the hours of working at present in Mr. Benyon's and Mr. Clayton's flax-mills?—Mr. Clayton's flax-mill is not going; Mr. Benyon's is going, but I do not know what hours they are working now.

Is not trade rather slack in that part of the country just now?—It is very slack at present.

While you were with Mr. Pearson, Mr. Giles and Mr. Chorley, you were in a better state of health?—Yes.

How old were you when you became a boiler in Mr. Brown's mill?—I believe I was about 20 years of age when I went to Mr. Brown.

You said you were a gigger at first?—That is, what I mean, when I became a boiler, I was somewhere about between 25 and 26.

You received 18 *s.* a week wages?—Yes.

Was that the regular wages without the extra hours, or did you receive more than 18 *s.* a week when you worked all these extra hours?—Yes.

How much did you ever receive?—I received 18: *s.* and over-hours, about 26 *s.* or 27 *s.* and sometimes 28 *s.*

At a regular charge of 3 *d.* an hour?—No, at 18 *s.* a week; it is 3-1/2 *d.* for all the hours over.

If you had not wasted these over-hours, you would not have been kept in your employment?—No, I should not have been kept in employ if I had not worked them.

Did not you and others choose to undergo this excessive labor, rather than incur the disgrace of throwing yourselves on the parish?—Yes.

You attended at the mill at five in the morning; was that both winter and summer?—It has been, for two years back, winter and summer, working at Mr. Brown's.

Were you able to be punctual in your attendance at five o'clock?—I was always there at five o'clock; if we were too late they took us off what we call bating; if we were a quarter of an hour too late in the morning they took off a penny.

Are they ever turned away for being too late?—If they are what is called "bad comers," they turn them off and get fresh ones.

Are they ever strapped for being too late?—They did not strap them at the room that I was in.

How did you contrive to be awake so soon in the morning?—My father always used to call me up.

Did he get up so early as that for his own business?—He got up on purpose to call me.

How many hours did he work in a day at his own business?—Sometimes from five in the morning till eight at night.

You say he was a shoemaker?—Yes.

Then, according to this, he worked more hours than you did?—I think not so long.

Did your father take his regular intervals for his meals?—I should think so.

And walked about to market for his family; had he not many pauses in his labour?—He worked at home, and therefore could do as he pleased.

After you worked a month at these long hours, could you not get back into lighter employment?—I do not know whether you could get back or not.

You said that you were about 17 when you first went from the flax-spinning mills into the cloth-mills?—Yes.

Was that before the Act of Parliament made to regulate the hours?—I know nothing about that.

How often did these extra hours come about?—Very often.

Describe to us a period in which you have worked the greatest possible number of hours; how many weeks running have you worked?—I have gone on for a year round.

Working all the Monday night and Friday night?—Yes; always working long hours.

Is your sister older or younger than yourself?—There is a year and a half between us; I am the elder.

Has your health improved since you left off working long hours?—I am a deal better than I was; but I believe that if I could have got work, and have had something to support me, I should have recruited my health better. I have been very poorly kept for these last six months, having been out of work. I have only half a crown a week allowed from the parish for my wife and myself.

When you were working the long hours, were there any people in the same employment, when you were a gigger, for instance, who were working the short hours?—Yes; some mills were working short hours in the same line; there were none in the same room that worked less hours than I did.

[*Joseph Hebergam examined.*] What particular department of the mill had you to attend to?—I attended what are called the throstle machines.

How long did you continue in that mill?—I attended the throstles two years and a half, and then I went to the steam looms for half a year.

Were there many children in that mill?—Yes, I believe there were about fifty, of about the same age that I was.

State to the Committee how this excessive labour agreed with the health of these children so employed?—They were often sick and poorly; there were always, perhaps, half a dozen regularly that were ill.

From excessive labour?—Yes.

Did you consider the work to be hard work?—It was not very hard, but having to work so very many hours made it worse; it was rather hard of itself, but it would have been better if we had not had so long to stand.

Did you not become very drowsy and sleepy towards the end of the day, and feel much fatigued?—Yes; that began about 3 o'clock, and grew worse and worse, and it came to be very bad towards 6 and 7.

And still you had to labour on?—Yes.

What means were taken to keep you at your work so long?—There were three overlookers; there was a head overlooker, and then there was one man kept to grease the machines, and then there was one kept on purpose to strap.

Was the main business of one of the overlookers that of strapping the children up to this excessive labour?—Yes, the same as strapping an old restive horse that has fallen down and will not get up.

Was that the constant practice?—Yes, day by day.

Were there straps regularly provided for that purpose?—Yes, he is continually walking up and down with it in his hand.

And his office is to strap you on to your labour?—Yes.

Do you think the children could be kept so long to labour as you have stated, if they were not so treated?—No, they could not; they are obliged to do it.

Was it not reckoned by the children to be very bad usage, and did they not conceive themselves to be very unfortunate in being subject to such a course of labour as this?—Yes; and towards the end of the day the flies of the machines would burst their knuckles.

Did you meet with frequent accidents?—Yes.

So that you were not capable of performing the labour that was exacted from you without this perpetual cruelty?—No.

Had you any brothers or sisters similarly occupied?—I had at that time a brother and a sister; they called him John, and my sister Charlotte.

What ages were they when they began working at the mills?—I cannot say how old my sister Charlotte was, but my brother John was 7.

How did it suit their health?—It did not suit it at all; they were often sick.

Where is your brother John working now?—He died three years ago.

What age was he when he died?—Sixteen years and eight months.

To what was his death attributed by your mother and the medical attendants?— It was attributed to this, that he died from working such long hours, and that it had been brought on by the factory. They have to stop the flies with their knees, because they go so swift they cannot stop them with their hands; he got a bruise on the shin by a spindle-board, and it went on to that degree that it burst; the surgeon cured that, then he was better; then he went to work again; but when he had worked about two months more his spine became affected, and he died.

Exploitation

E. P. Thompson

E. P. Thompson (1924–1993) was a prominent British historian, socialist leader, and peace advocate. His The Making of the English Working Class (1963), *from which this is an excerpt, has been hailed as a classic work of social history, and is still regarded as an authoritative work on the impact of industrialization on the British class system.*

For most working people the crucial experience of the Industrial Revolution was felt in terms of changes in the nature and intensity of exploitation. Nor is this some anachronistic notion, imposed upon the evidence. We may describe some parts of the exploitive process as they appeared to one remarkable cotton operative in 1818—the year in which Marx was born. The account—an Address to the public of strike-bound Manchester by "A Journeyman Cotton Spinner"—commences by describing the employers and the workers as "two distinct classes of persons":

"First, then, as to the employers: with very few exceptions, they are a set of men who have sprung from the cotton-shop without education or address, except so much as they have acquired by their intercourse with the little world of merchants on the exchange at Manchester; but to counterbalance that deficiency, they give you enough of appearances by an ostentatious display of elegant mansions, equipages, liveries, parks, hunters, hounds, etc., which they take care to shew off to the merchant stranger in the most pompous manner. Indeed their houses are gorgeous palaces, far surpassing in bulk and extent the neat charming retreats you see round London . . . but the chaste observer of the beauties of nature and art combined will observe a woeful deficiency of taste. They bring up their families at the most costly schools, determined to give their offspring a double portion of what they were so deficient in themselves. Thus with scarcely a second idea in their heads, they are literally petty monarchs, absolute and despotic, in their own particular districts; and to support all this, their whole time is occupied in contriving how to get the greatest quantity of work turned off with the least expense. . . . In short, I will venture to say, without fear of contradiction, that there is a greater distance observed between the master there and the spinner, than there is between the first merchant in London and his lowest servant or the lowest artisan. Indeed there is no comparison. I know it to be a fact, that the greater part of the master spinners are anxious to keep wages low for the purpose of keeping the spinners indigent and spiritless . . . as for the purpose of taking the surplus to their own pockets."

"The master spinners are a class of men unlike all other master tradesmen in the kingdom. They are ignorant, proud, and tyrannical. What then must be the men or rather beings who are the instruments of such masters? Why, they have been for a series of years, with their wives and their families, patience itself—bondmen and bondwomen to their duel taskmasters. It is in vain to insult our common understandings with the observation that such men are free; that the law protects the rich and poor alike, and that a spinner can leave his master if he does not like the wages. True; so he can: but where must he go? why to another, to be sure. Well: he goes; he is asked where did you work last: 'Did he discharge you?' No; we could not agree about wages. Well I shall not employ you nor anyone who leaves his master in that manner. Why is this? Because there is an abominable *combination existing amongst the masters*, first established at Stockport in 1802, and it has since become so general, as to embrace all the great masters for a circuit of many miles round Manchester, though not the little masters: they are excluded. They are the most obnoxious beings to the great ones that can be imagined. . . . When the combination first took place, one of their first articles was, that no master should take on a man until he had first ascertained whether his last master had discharged him. What then is the man to do? If he goes to the parish, that grave of all independence, he is there told—We shall not relieve you; if you dispute with your master, and don't support your family, we will send you to prison; so that the man is bound, by a combination of circumstances, to submit to his master. He cannot travel and get work in any town like a shoe-maker, joiner, or taylor; he is confined to the district."

"The workmen in general are an inoffensive, unassuming, set of well-informed men, though how they acquire their information is almost a mystery to me. They are docile and tractable, if not goaded too much; but this is not to be wondered at, when we consider that they are trained to work from six years old from five in a morning to eight and nine at night. Let one of the advocates for obedience to his master take his stand in an avenue leading to a factory a little before five o'clock in the morning, and observe the squalid appearance of the little infants and their parents taken from their beds at so early an hour in all kinds of weather; let him examine the miserable pittance of food, chiefly composed of water gruel and oatcake broken into it, a little salt, and sometimes colored with a little milk, together with a few potatoes, and a bit of bacon or fat for dinner; would a London mechanic eat this? There they are, (and if late a few minutes, a quarter of a day is stopped in wages) locked up until night in rooms heated above the hottest days we have had this summer, and allowed no time, except three-quarters of an hour at dinner in the whole day: whatever they eat at any other time must be as they are at work. The negro slave in the West Indies, if he works under a scorching sun, has probably a little breeze of air sometimes to fan him: he has a space of ground, and time allowed to cultivate it. The English spinner slave has no enjoyment of the open atmosphere and breezes of heaven. Locked up in factories eight stories high, he has no relaxation till the ponderous engine stops, and then he goes home to get refreshed for the next day; no time for sweet association with his family; they are all alike fatigued and exhausted. This is no over-drawn picture: it is literally true. I ask again, would the mechanics in the South of England submit to this?"

"When the spinning of cotton was in its infancy, and before those terrible machines for superseding the necessity of human labour, called steam engines, came into use, there were a great number of what were then called *little masters*; men who with a small capital, could procure a few machines, and employ a few hands, men and boys (say to twenty or thirty), the produce of whose labour was all taken to Manchester central mart, and put into the hands of brokers. . . . The brokers sold it to the merchants, by which means the master spinner was enabled to stay at home and work and attend to his workmen. The cotton was then always given out in its raw state from the bale to the wives of the spinners at home, when they heat and cleansed it ready for the spinners in the factory. By this they could earn eight, ten, or twelve shillings a week, and cook and attend to their families. But none are thus employed now; for all the cotton is broke up by a machine, turned by the steam engine, called a devil: so that the spinners' wives have no employment, except they go to work in the factory all day at what can be done by children for a few shillings, four or five per week. If a man then could not agree with his master, he left him, and could get employed elsewhere. A few years, however, changed the face of things. Steam engines came into use, to purchase which, and to erect buildings sufficient to contain them and six or seven hundred hands, required a great capital. The engine power produced a more marketable (though not a better) article than the little master could at the same price. The consequence was their ruin in a short time; and the overgrown capitalists triumphed in their fall; for they were the only obstacle that stood between them and the complete control of the workmen."

"Various disputes then originated between the workmen and masters as to the fineness of the work, the workmen being paid according to the number of hanks or yards of thread he produce from a given quantity of cotton, which was always to be proved by the overlooker, whose interest made it imperative on him to lean to his master, and call the material coarser than it was. If the workman would not submit *he must summon his employer before a magistrate*; the whole of the acting magistrates in that district, with the exception of two worthy clergymen, being gentlemen who have sprung from the *same* source with the master cotton spinners. The employer generally contented himself with sending his overlooker to answer any such summons, thinking it beneath him to meet his servant. The magistrate's decision was generally in favour of the master, though on the statement of the overlooker only. The workman dared not appeal to the sessions on account of the expense . . ."

"These evils to the men have arisen from that dreadful monopoly which exists in those districts where wealth and power are got into the hands of the few, who, in the pride of their hearts, think themselves the lords of the universe."[1]

This reading of the facts, in its remarkable cogency, is as much an *ex parte* statement as is the "political economy" of Lord Brougham. But the "Journeyman Cotton Spinner" was describing facts of a different order. We need not concern ourselves with the soundness of all his judgements. What his address does is to itemize one after another the grievances felt by working people as to changes in the character of capitalist exploitation: the rise of a master-class without traditional authority or obligations: the growing distance between master and man: the transparency of the exploitation at the source of their new wealth and power: the loss of status and above all of independence for the worker, his reduction to total dependence on the master's instruments of production: the partiality of the law: the disruption of the traditional family economy: the discipline, monotony, hours and conditions of work: loss of leisure and amenities: the reduction of the man to the status of an "instrument."

That working people felt these grievances at all—and felt them passionately—is itself a sufficient fact to merit our attention. And it reminds us forcibly that some of the most bitter conflicts of these years turned on issues which are not encompassed by cost-of-living series. The issues which provoked the most intensity of feeling were very often ones in which such values as traditional customs, "justice," "independence," security, or family-economy were at stake, rather than straight-forward bread-and-butter issues. The early years of the 1830s are aflame with agitations which turned on issues in which wages were of secondary importance; by the potters, against the Truck System; by the textile workers, for the 10-Hour Bill; by the building workers, for cooperative direct action; by all groups of workers, for the right to join trade unions. The great strike in the north-east coalfield in 1831 turned on security of employment, "tommy shops," child labour.

The exploitive relationship is more than the sum of grievances and mutual antagonisms. It is a relationship which can be seen to take distinct forms in different historical contexts, forms which are related to corresponding forms of ownership and State power. The classic exploitive relationship of the Industrial Revolution is depersonalized, in the sense that no lingering obligations of mutuality—of paternalism or deference, or of the interests of "the Trade"—are admitted. There is no whisper of the "just" price, or of a wage justified in relation to social or moral sanctions, as opposed to the operation of free market forces. Antagonism is accepted as intrinsic to the relations of production. Managerial or supervisory functions demand the repression of all attributes except those which further the expropriation of the maximum surplus value from labour. This is the political economy which Marx anatomized in *Das Kapital*. The worker has become an "instrument," or an entry among other items of cost.

In fact, no complex industrial enterprise could be conducted according to such a philosophy. The need for industrial peace, for a stable labour-force, and for a body of skilled and experienced workers, necessitated the modification of managerial techniques—and, indeed, the growth of new forms of paternalism—in the cotton-mills by the 1830s. But in the overstocked outwork industries, where there was always a sufficiency of unorganized "hands" competing for employment, these considerations did not operate. Here, as old customs were eroded, and old paternalism was set aside, the exploitive relationship emerged supreme. . . .

These larger considerations have been, for some years, overlaid by the academic exercise (through which all students must march and counter-march) known as the "standard-of-living controversy." Did the living standards of the bulk of the people rise or fall between 1780 and 1830—or 1800 and 1850?[2] . . .

In fact, so far as the period 1790–1830 goes, there is very little in it. The condition of the majority was bad in 1790: it remained bad in 1830 (and forty years is a long time) but there is some disagreement as to the size of the relative groups within the working class. And matters are little clearer in the next decade. There were undoubted increases in real wages among organized workers during the burst of trade union activity between 1832–4: but the period of good trade between 1833 and 1837 was accompanied by the smashing of the trade unions by the concerted efforts of Government, magistrates, and employers; while 1837–42 are depression years. So that it is indeed at "some unspecified date between the drafting of the People's Charter and the Great Exhibition" that the tide begins to turn; let us say, with the railway boom in 1843. Moreover, even in the mid-40s the plight of very large groups of workers remains desperate, while the railway crash led to the depression years of 1847–8. This does not look very much like a "success story"; in half a century of the fullest development of industrialism, the standard-of-living still remained—for very large but indeterminate groups—at the point of subsistence. . . .

The controversy falls into two parts. There is, first, the very real difficulty of constructing wage-series, price-series, and statistical indices from the abundant but patchy evidence. We shall examine some of the difficulties in interpreting such evidence when we come to the artisans. But at this point a further series of difficulties begins, since the term standard leads us from date amenable to statistical measurement (wages or articles of consumption) to those satisfactions which are sometimes described by statisticians as "imponderables." From food we are led to homes, from homes to health, from health to family life, and thence to leisure, work-discipline, education and play, intensity of labour, and so on. From standard-of-life we pass to way-of-life. But the two are not the same. The first is a measurement of quantities: the second a description (and sometimes an evaluation) of qualities. Where statistical evidence is appropriate to the first, we must rely largely upon "literary evidence" as to the second. A major source of confusion arises from the drawing of conclusions as to one from evidence appropriate only to the other. It is at times as if statisticians have been arguing: "the indices reveal an increased *per capita* consumption of tea, sugar, meat and soap, *therefore* the working class was happier," while social historians have replied: "the literary sources show that people were unhappy, *therefore* their standard-of-living must have deteriorated."

This is to simplify. But simple points must be made. It is quite possible for statistical averages and human experiences to run in opposite directions. A *per capita* increase in quantitative factors may take place at the same time as a great qualitative disturbance in people's way of life, traditional relationships, and sanctions. People may consume more goods and become less happy or less free at the same time. Next to the agricultural workers the largest single group of working people during the whole period of the Industrial Revolution were the domestic servants. Very many of them were household servants, living-in with the employing family, sharing cramped quarters, working excessive hours, for a few shillings' reward. Nevertheless, we may confidently list them among the more favoured groups whose standards (or consumption of food and dress) improved on average slightly during the Industrial Revolution. But the handloom weaver and his wife, on the edge of starvation, still regarded their status as being superior to that of "flunkey." Or again, we might cite those trades, such as coal-mining, in which real wages advanced between 1790 and 1840, but at the cost of longer hours and a greater intensity of labour, so that the breadwinner was "worn out" before the age of forty. In statistical terms, this reveals an upward curve. To the families concerned it might feel like immiseration.

Thus it is perfectly possible to maintain two propositions which, on a casual view, appear to be contradictory. Over the period 1790–1840 there was a slight improvement in average material standards. Over the same period there was intensified exploitation, greater insecurity, and increasing human misery. By 1840 most people were "better off" than their forerunners had been fifty years before, but they had suffered and continued to suffer this slight improvement as a catastrophic experience.

Notes

1. *Black Dwarf*, 30 September 1818.

2. The futility of one part of this discussion is shown by the fact that if different datum-lines are taken, different answers may come up. 1780–1830 favours the "pessimists"; 1800–1850 favours the "optimists."

On Liberty

John Stuart Mill

Mill's On Liberty (1859) *is perhaps the most influential and persuasive explication of the principles of Classical Liberalism. His impassioned arguments concerning the extent and limitations of individual freedom, and the importance of free expression, are still considered essential components of most modern democratic governments.*

Chapter I: Introductory

. . . The struggle between Liberty and Authority is the most conspicuous feature in the portions of history with which we are earliest familiar, particularly in that of Greece, Rome, and England. But in old times this contest was between subjects, or some classes of subjects, and the Government. By liberty was meant protection against the tyranny of the political rulers. The rulers were conceived (except in some of the popular governments of Greece) as in a necessarily antagonistic position to the people whom they ruled. . . .

A time, however, came in the progress of human affairs when men ceased to think it a necessity of nature that their governors should be an independent power, opposed in interest to themselves. It appeared to them much better that the various magistrates of the State should be their tenants or delegates, revocable at their pleasure. In that way alone, it seemed, could they have complete security that the powers of government would never be abused to their disadvantage. By degrees this new demand for elective and temporary rulers became the prominent object of the exertions of the popular party, wherever any such party existed; and superseded to a considerable extent, the previous efforts to limit the power of rulers. As the struggle proceeded for making the ruling power emanate from the periodical choice of the ruled, some persons began to think that too much importance had been attached to the limitation of the power itself. That (it might seem) was a resource against rulers whose interests were habitually opposed to those of the people. What was now wanted was, that the rulers should be identified with the people; that their interest and will should be in the interest and will of the nation. The nation did not need to be protected against its own will. There was no fear of its tyrannizing over itself. Let the rulers be effectually responsible to it, promptly removable by it, and it could afford to trust them with power of which it could itself dictate the use to be made. Their power was but the nation's own power, concentrated, and in a form convenient for exercise. This mode of thought, or rather perhaps of feeling, was common among the last generation of European Liberalism, in the Continental section of which it still apparently predominates. Those who admit any limit to what a government may do, except in the case of such governments as they think ought not to exist, stand out as brilliant exceptions among the political thinkers of the Continent. A similar tone of sentiment might by this time have been prevalent in our own country, if the circumstances which for a time encouraged it had continued unaltered.

But, in political and philosophical theories, as well as in persons, success discloses faults and infirmities which failure might have concealed from observation. The notion, that the people have no need to limit their power over themselves, might seem axiomatic when popular government was a thing only dreamed about, or read of as having existed at some distant period of the past. Neither was that notion necessarily disturbed by such temporary aberrations as those of the French Revolution, the worst of which were the work of an usurping few, and which, in any case, belonged not to the permanent working of popular institutions, but to a sudden and convulsive outbreak against monarchical and aristocratic despotism. In time, however, a democratic republic came to occupy a large portion of the earth's surface, and made itself felt as one of the most powerful members of the community of nations; and elective and responsible government became subject to the observations and criticisms which wait upon a great existing fact. It was now perceived that such phrases as "self-government," and "the power of the people over themselves," do not express the true state of the case. The "people" who exercise the power are not always the same people with those over whom it is exercised; and the "self-government" spoken of is not the government of each by himself, but of each by all the rest. The will of the people, moreover, practically means the will of the most numerous or the most active part of the people; the majority, or those who succeed in making themselves accepted as the majority; the people, consequently, may desire to oppress a part of their number, and precautions are as much needed against any other abuse of power. The limitation, therefore, of the power of government over individuals loses none of its importance when the holders of power are regularly accountable to the community, that is, to the strongest party therein. This view of things, recommending itself equally to the intelligence of thinkers and to the inclination of those important classes in European society to whose real or supposed interests democracy is adverse, has had no difficulty in establishing itself; and in political speculations "the tyranny of the majority" is now generally included among the evils against which society requires to be on its guard. . . .

Chapter II: Of the Liberty of Thought and Discussion

The time, it is to be hoped, is gone by, when any defense would be necessary of the "liberty of the press" as one of the securities against corrupt or tyrannical government. No argument, we may suppose, can now be needed, against permitting a legislature or an executive, not identified in interest with the people, to prescribe opinions to them, and determine what doctrines or what arguments, they shall be allowed to hear . . . Let us suppose, therefore, that the government is entirely at one with the people, and never thinks of exerting any power of coercion unless in agreement with what it conceives to be their voice. But I deny the right of the people to exercise such coercion, either by themselves or by their government. The power itself is illegitimate. The best government has no more title to it than the worst. It is as noxious, or more noxious, when exerted in accordance with public opinion, than when in opposition to it. If all mankind minus one, were of one opinion, and only one person were of the contrary opinion, mankind would be no more justified in silencing that one person, than he, if he had the power, would be justified in silencing mankind. Were an opinion a personal possession of no value except to the owner; if to be obstructed in the enjoyment of it were simply a private injury, it would make some difference whether the injury was inflicted only on a few persons or on many. But the peculiar evil of silencing the expression of an opinion is that it is robbing the human race; posterity as well as the existing generation; those who dissent from the opinion, still more than those who hold it. If the opinion is right, they are deprived of the opportunity of exchanging error for truth: if wrong, they lose, what is almost as great a benefit, the clearer perception and livelier impression of truth, produced by its collision with error.

It is necessary to consider separately these two hypotheses, each of which has a distinct branch of the argument corresponding to it. We can never be sure that the opinion we are endeavoring to stifle is false opinion; and if we were sure, stifling it would be an evil still . . .

We have recognized the necessity to the mental well-being of mankind (on which all their other well-being depends) of freedom of opinion, and freedom of the expression of opinion, on four distinct grounds; which we will now briefly recapitulate.

First, if any opinion is compelled to silence, that opinion may, for aught we can certainly know, be true. To deny this is to assume our own infallibility.

Secondly, though the silenced opinion be an error, it may, and very commonly does, contain a portion of truth; and since the general or prevailing opinion on any subject is rarely or never the whole truth, it is only by the collision of adverse opinions that the remainder of the truth has any chance of being supplied.

Thirdly, even if the received opinion be not only true, but the whole truth; unless it is suffered to be, and actually is, vigorously and earnestly contested, it will, by most of those who receive it, be held in the manner of a prejudice, with little comprehension or feeling of its rational grounds. And not only this, but, fourthly, the meaning of the doctrine itself will be in danger of being lost, or enfeebled, and deprived of its vital effect on the character and conduct: the dogma becoming a mere formal profession, inefficacious for good, but cumbering the ground, and preventing the growth of any real and heartfelt conviction, from reason or personal experience . . .

Chapter III: Of Individuality, As One of the Elements of Well Being

Such being the reasons which make it imperative that human beings should be free to form opinions, and to express their opinions without reserve; and such the baneful consequences to the intellectual, and through that to the moral nature of man, unless this liberty is either conceded, or asserted in spite of prohibition; let us next examine whether the same reasons do not require that men should be free to act upon their opinions—to carry these out in their lives, without hindrance, either physical or moral, from their fellow men, so long as it is at their own risk and peril. This last proviso is, of course, indispensable. No one pretends that actions should be as free as opinions. On the contrary, even opinions lose their immunity, when the circumstances in which they are expressed are such as to constitute their expression a positive instigation to some mischievous act. An opinion that corn dealers are starvers of the poor, or that private property is robbery, ought to be unmolested when simply circulated through the press, but may justly incur punishment when delivered orally to an excited mob assembled before the house of a corn dealer, or when handed about among the same mob in the form of a placard. Acts, of whatever kind, which, without justifiable cause, do harm to others, may be, and in the more important cases absolutely require to be, controlled by the unfavorable sentiments, and, when needful, by the active interference of mankind. The liberty of the individual must be thus far limited; he must not make himself a nuisance to other people. But if he refrains from molesting others in what concerns them, and merely acts according to his own inclination and judgment in things which concern himself, the same reasons which show that opinion should be free, prove also that he should be allowed, without molestation, to carry his opinions into practice at his own cost. That mankind are not infallible; that their truths, for the most part, are only half-truths; that unity of opinion, unless resulting from the fullest and freest comparison of opposite opinions, is not desirable, and diversity not an evil, but a good, until mankind are much more capable than at present of recognizing all sides of the truth, are principles applicable to men's modes of action, not less than to their opinions. As it is useful that while mankind are imperfect there should be different opinions, so is it that there should be different experiments of living; that free scope should be given varieties of character, short of injury to others; and that the worth of different modes of life should be proved practically, when any one thinks fit to try them. It is desirable, in short, that in things which do not primarily concern others, individuality should assert itself. Where, not the person's own character, but the traditions or customs of other people are the rule of conduct, there is wanting one of the principal ingredients of human happiness, and quite the chief ingredient of individual and social progress . . . No one's idea of excellence in conduct is that people should do absolutely nothing but copy one another. No one would assert that people ought not to put into their mode of life, and into the conduct of their concerns, any impress whatever of their own judgment, or of their own individual character. On the other hand, it would be absurd to pretend that people ought to live as if nothing whatever had been known in the world before they came into it; as if experience had as yet done nothing towards showing that one mode of existence, or of conduct, is preferable to another. Nobody denies that people should be so taught and trained in youth, as to know and benefit by the ascertained results of human experience. But it is the privilege and proper condition of a human being, arrived at the maturity of his faculties, to use and interpret experience in his own way. It is for him to find out what part of recorded experience is properly applicable to his own circumstances and character. The traditions and customs of other people are, to certain extent, evidence of what their experience has taught them; presumptive evidence, and as such, have a claim to his deference; but, in the first place, their experience may be too narrow; or they may not have interpreted it rightly. Secondly, their interpretation of experience may be correct, but unsuitable to him. Customs are made for customary circumstances, and customary characters; and his circumstances or his character may be uncustomary. Thirdly, though the customs be both good as customs, and suitable to him, yet to conform to custom, merely as custom, does not educate or develop in him any of the qualities which are the distinctive endowment of a human being. The human faculties of perception, judgment, discriminative feeling, mental activity, and even moral preference, are exercised only in making a choice. He who does anything because it is the custom, makes no choice. He gains no practice either in discerning or in desiring what is best. The mental and moral, like the muscular powers, are improved only by being used. The faculties are called into no exercise by doing a thing merely because others do it, no more than by believing a thing only because others believe it. If the groups of opinion are not conclusive to the person's own reason, his reason cannot be strengthened, but is likely to be weakened, by his adopting it: and if the inducements to an act are not such as are consentaneous to his own feelings and character (where affection, or the rights of others, are not concerned) it is so much done towards rendering his feelings and character inert and torpid, instead of active and energetic . . .

Chapter V: Applications

. . . I offer not so much applications as specimens of application; which may serve to bring into greater clearness the meaning and limits of the two maxims which together form the entire doctrine of the Essay, and to assist the judgment in holding the balance between them, in the cases where it appears doubtful which of them is applicable to the case.

The maxims are, first, that the individual is not accountable to society for his actions, in so far as these concern the interests of no person but himself. Advice, instruction, persuasion, and avoidance by other people of thought necessary by them for their own good, are the only measures by which society can justifiably express its dislike or disapprobation of his conduct. Secondly, that for such actions as are prejudicial to the interests of others, the individual is accountable, and may be subjected either to social or to legal punishment, if society is of opinion that the one or the other is requisite for its protection.

In the first place, it must by no means be supposed, because damage, or probability of damage, to the interests of others, can alone justify the interference of society, that therefore it always does justify such interference. In many cases, an individual, in pursuing a legitimate object, necessarily and therefore legitimately causes pain or loss to others, or intercepts a good which they have a reasonable hope of obtaining. Such oppositions of interest between individuals often arise from bad social institutions, but are unavoidable while those institutions last; and some would be unavoidable under any institutions. Whoever succeeds in an over-crowded profession, or in a competitive examination; whoever is preferred to another in any contest for an object which both desire, reaps benefit from the loss of others, from their wasted exertion and their disappointment. But it is, by common admission, better for the general interest of mankind, that persons should pursue their objects undeterred by this sort of consequence. In other words, society admits no right, either legal or moral, in the disappointed competitors, to immunity from this kind of suffering; and feels called on to interfere, only when means of success have been employed which it is contrary to the general interest to permit—namely, fraud or treachery, and force.

Again, trade is a social act. Whoever undertakes to sell any description of goods to the public, does what affects the interest of other persons, and of society in general; and thus his conduct, in principle comes within the jurisdiction of society: accordingly, it was once held to be the duty of governments, in all cases which were considered of importance, to fix prices, and regulate the processes of manufacture. But it is now recognized, though not till after a long struggle, that both the cheapness and the good quality of commodities are most effectually provided for by leaving the producers and sellers perfectly free, under the sole check of equal freedom to the buyers for supplying themselves elsewhere. This is the so-called doctrine of Free Trade, which rests on grounds different from, though equally solid with, the principle of individual liberty asserted in this essay. Restrictions on trade, or on production for purposes of trade, are indeed restraints; and all restraint, *quo* restraint, is an evil: but the restraints in question affect only the part of conduct which society is competent to restrain, and are wrong solely because they do not really produce the results which it is desired to produce by them. . . . It is one of the undisputed functions of government to take precautions against crime before it has been committed, as well as to detect and punish it afterwards. The preventive function of government, however, is far more liable to be abused, to the prejudice of liberty, than the punitory function; for there is hardly any part of the legitimate freedom of action of a human being which would not admit of being represented, and fairly too, as increasing the facilities for some form or other of delinquency. Nevertheless, if a public authority, or even a private person, sees anyone evidently preparing to commit a crime, they are not bound to look on inactive until the crime is committed, but may interfere to prevent it. If poisons were never bought or used for any purpose except the commission of murder it would be right to prohibit their manufacture and sale. They may, however, be wanted not only for innocent but for useful purposes, and restrictions cannot be imposed in the one case without operating in the other. Again, it is a proper office of public authority to guard against accidents. If either a public officer or anyone else saw a person attempting to cross a bridge which had been ascertained to be unsafe, and there were no time to warn him of his danger, they might seize him and turn him back, without any real infringement of his liberty; for liberty consists in doing what one desires, and he does not desire to fall into the river. Nevertheless, when there is not a certainty, but only a danger of mischief, no one but the person himself can judge of the sufficiency of the motive which may prompt him to incur the risk: in this case, therefore (unless he is a child, or delirious, or in some state of excitement or absorption incompatible with the full use of the reflecting faculty), he ought, I conceive, to be only warned of the danger; not forcibly prevented from exposing himself to it. . . .

The right inherent in society to ward off crimes against itself by antecedent precautions, suggests the obvious limitations to the maxim, that purely self-regarding misconduct cannot properly be meddled with in the way of prevention or punishment. Drunkenness, for example, in ordinary cases, is not a fit subject for legislative interference; but I should deem it perfectly legitimate that a person who had once been convicted of any act of violence to others under the influence of drink, should be placed under a special legal restriction, personal to himself; that if he were afterwards found drunk, he should be liable to a penalty, and that if when in that state he committed another offense, the punishment to which he would be liable for that other offense should be increased in severity. The making himself drunk, in a person whom drunkenness excites to do harm to others, is a crime against others. So, again, idleness, except in a person receiving support from the public, or except when it constitutes a breach of contract, cannot without tyranny be made a subject of legal punishment; but if, either from idleness or from any other avoidable cause, a man fails to perform his legal duties to others, as for instance to support his children, it is no tyranny to force him to fulfill that obligation, by compulsory labour, if no other means are available. . . .

I have already observed that, owing to the absence of any recognized general principles, liberty is often granted where it should be withheld, as well as withheld where it should be granted; and one of the cases in which, in the modern European world the sentiment of liberty is the strongest, is a case where, in my view, it is altogether misplaced. A person should be free to do as he likes in his own concerns; but he ought not to be free to do as he likes in acting for another, under the pretext that the affairs of the other are his own affairs. The State, while it respects the liberty of each in what specially regards himself, is bound to maintain a vigilant control over his exercise of any power which it allows him to possess over others. This obligation is almost entirely disregarded in the case of the family relations, a case, in its direct influence on human happiness, more important than all others taken together. The almost despotic power of husbands over wives need not be enlarged upon here, because nothing more is needed for the complete removal of the veil, than that wives should have the same rights, and should receive the protection of law in the same manner, as all other persons; and because, on this subject, the defenders of established injustice do not avail themselves of the plea of liberty, but stand forth openly as the champions of power. It is in the case of children, that misapplied notions of liberty are a real obstacle to the fulfillment by the State of its duties. One would almost think that a man's children were supposed to be literally, and not metaphorically, a part of himself, so jealous is opinion of the smallest interference of law with his absolute and exclusive control over them; more jealous than of almost any interference with his own freedom of action; so much less do the generality of mankind value liberty than power. Consider, for example, the case of education. Is it not almost a self-evident axiom, that the State should require and compel the education, up to a certain standard, of every human being who is born its citizen? Yet who is there that is not afraid to recognize and assert this truth? Hardly any one indeed will deny that it is one of the most sacred duties of the parents (or, as law and usage now stand, the father), after summoning a human being into the world, to give to that being an education fitting him to perform his part well in life towards others and towards himself. But while this is unanimously declared to be the father's duty, scarcely anybody, in this country, will bear to hear of obliging him to perform it. Instead of his being required to make any exertion or sacrifice for securing education to the child, it is left to his choice to accept it or not when it is provided *gratis!* It still remains unrecognized that to bring a child into existence without a fair prospect of being able, not only to provide food for its body, but instruction and training for its mind, is a moral crime, both against the unfortunate offspring and against society; and that if the parent does not fulfill this obligation, the State ought to see it fulfilled, at the charge, as far as possible, of the parent. . . .

It is not a matter of education only, that misplaced notions of liberty prevent moral obligations on the part of parents from being recognized, and legal obligations from being imposed, where there are the strongest grounds for the former always, and in many cases for the latter also. The fact itself, of causing the existence of a human being, is one of the most responsible actions in the range of human life. To undertake this responsibility—to bestow a life which may be either a curse or a blessing—unless the being on whom it is to be bestowed will have at least the ordinary chances of a desirable existence, is a crime against that being. And in a country either over-peopled, or threatened with being so, to produce children, beyond a very small number, with the effect of reducing the regard of labour by their competition, is a serious offense against all who live by the remuneration of their labour. The laws which, in many countries on the Continent, forbid marriage unless the parties can show that they have the means of supporting a family, do not exceed the legitimate powers of the State: and whether such laws be expedient or not (a question mainly dependent on local circumstances and feelings), they are not objectionable as violations of liberty. Such laws are interferences of the State to prohibit a mischievous act—an act injurious to others, which ought to be a subject of reprobation, and social stigma, even when it is not deemed expedient to superadd legal punishment. Yet the current ideas of liberty, which bend so easily to real infringements of the freedom of the individual in things which concern only himself, would repel the attempt to put any restraint upon his inclinations when the consequence of their indulgence is a life or lives of wretchedness and depravity to the offspring, with manifold evils to those sufficiently within reach to be in any way affected by their actions. When we compare the strange respect of mankind for liberty, with their strange want of respect for it, we might imagine that a man had an indispensable right to do harm to others, and no right at all to please himself without giving pain to anyone.

I have reserved for the last place a large class of questions respecting the limits of government interference, which, though closely connected with the subject of this Essay, do not, in strictness, belong to it. These are cases in which the reasons against interference do not turn upon the principle of liberty; the question is not about restraining the actions of individuals, but about helping them; it is asked whether the government should do, or cause to be done, something for their benefit, instead of leaving it to be done by themselves, individually or in voluntary combination.

The objections to government interference, when it is not such as to involve infringement of liberty, may be of three kinds.

The first is, when the thing to be done is likely to be better done by individuals than by the government. Speaking generally, there is no one so fit to conduct any business, or to determine how or by whom it shall be conducted, as those who are personally interested in it. This principle condemns the interferences, once so common, of the legislature, or the officers of government, with the ordinary processes of industry. But this part of the subject has been sufficiently enlarged upon by political economists, and is not particularly related to the principles of this Essay.

The second objection is more nearly allied to our subject. In many cases, though individuals may not do the particular thing so well, on the average, as the officers of government, it is nevertheless desirable that it should be done by them rather than by the government, as a means to their own mental education—a mode of strengthening their active faculties, exercising their judgment, and giving them a familiar knowledge of the subjects with which they are thus left to deal. This is a principal, though not the sole, recommendation of jury trial (in cases not political); of free and popular local and municipal institutions; of the conduct of industrial and philanthropic enterprises by voluntary associations. These are not questions of liberty, and are connected with that subject only by remote tendencies; but they are questions of development. It belongs to a different occasion from the present to dwell on these things as parts of national education; as being, in truth, the peculiar training of a citizen, the practical part of the political education of a free people, taking them out of the narrow circle of personal and family selfishness, and accustoming them to the comprehension of joint interests, the management of joint concerns—habituating them to act from public or semi-public motives, and guide their conduct by aims which unite instead of isolating them from one another. Without these habits and powers, a free constitution can neither be worked nor preserved; as is exemplified by the too-often transitory nature of political freedom in countries where it does not rest upon a sufficient basis of local liberties. The management of purely local business by the localities, and of the great enterprises of industry by the union of those who voluntarily supply the pecuniary means, is further recommended by all the advantages which have been set forth in this Essay as belonging to individuality of development, and diversity of modes of action. Government operations tend to be everywhere alike. With individuals and voluntary associations, on the contrary, there are varied experiments, and endless diversity of experience. What the State can usefully do is make itself a central depository, and active circulator and diffuser, of the experience resulting from many trials. Its business is to enable each experimentalist to benefit by the experiments of others, instead of tolerating no experiments but its own.

The third and most cogent reason for restricting the interferences of government, is the great evil of adding unnecessarily to its power. Every function superadded to those already exercised by the government causes its influence over hopes and fears to be more widely diffused, and converts, more and more, the active and ambitious part of the public into hangers-on of the government, or of some part which aims at becoming the government. If the roads, the railways, the banks, the insurance offices, the great joint-stock companies, the universities, and the public charities, were all of them branches of the government; if, in addition, the municipal corporations and local boards, with all that now devolves on them, became departments of the central administration; if the employees of all these different enterprises were appointed and paid by the government, and looked to the government for every rise in life; not all the freedom of the press and popular constitution of the legislature would make this or any other country free otherwise than in name. And the evil would be greater, the more efficiently and scientifically the administrative machinery was constructed—

the more skillful the arrangements for obtaining the best qualified hands and heads with which to work it.

If every part of the business of society which required organized concert, or large and comprehensive views, were in the hands of the government, and if government offices were universally filled by the ablest men, all the enlarged culture and practiced intelligence in the country, except the purely speculative, would be concentrated in a numerous bureaucracy, to whom alone the rest of the community would look for all things: the multitude for direction and dictation in all they had to do; the able and aspiring for personal advancement. To be admitted into the ranks of this bureaucracy, and when admitted, to rise therein, would be the sole objects of ambition. Under this regime, not only is the outside public ill-qualified, for want of practical experience, to criticize or check the mode of operation of the bureaucracy, but even if the accidents of despotic or the natural working of popular institutions occasionally raise to the summit a ruler or rulers of reforming inclinations, no reform can be effected which is contrary to the interest of the bureaucracy. Such is the melancholy condition of the Russian empire, as shown in the accounts of those who have had sufficient opportunity of observation. The Czar himself is powerless against the bureaucratic body; he can send any one of them to Siberia, but he cannot govern without them, or against their will. On every decree of his they have a tacit veto, by merely refraining from carrying it into effect. In countries of more advanced civilization and of a more insurrectionary spirit, the public, accustomed to expect everything to be done for them by the State, or at least to do nothing for themselves without asking from the State not only leave to do it, but even how it is to be done, naturally hold the State responsible for all evil which befalls them, and when the evil exceeds their amount of patience, they rise against the government, and make what is called a revolution; whereupon somebody else, with or without legitimate authority from the nation, vaults into the seat, issues his orders to the bureaucracy, and everything goes on much as it did before; the bureaucracy being unchanged, and nobody else being capable of taking their place. . . .

Nations and Nationalism

Heinrich von Treitschke

It is not suggested that the following selection was connected directly with Darwinism. The new bellicose nationalism and racism were, however, contemporary with, and flourished in, the Darwinian world. Nor should it be inferred that they were peculiar to Germans. Nevertheless, Heinrich von Treitschke (1834–96), historian and university professor, was one of the chief exponents of the new nationalism. A liberal in his youth, he devoted his mature years to extolling the mission of Prussia to unify Germany and of Bismarck's united Germany to lead Europe and the world. His magnum opus was his History of Germany in the Nineteenth Century *(first volume 1879). The following selections are from his lectures on politics and the state, delivered at Berlin in the 1880s and 1890s.*

The State is the people, legally united as an independent entity. By the word "people" we understand briefly a number of families permanently living side by side. This definition implies that the State is primordial and necessary, that it is as enduring as history, and no less essential to mankind than speech. History, however, begins for us with the art of writing; earlier than this men's conscious recollection of the past cannot be reckoned with. Therefore everything which lies beyond this limit is rightly judged to be prehistoric. We, on the other hand, must deal here with man as an historical being, and we can only say that creative political genius is inherent in him, and that the State, like him, subsists from the beginning. The attempt to present it as something artificial, following upon a natural condition, has fallen completely into discredit. We lack all historical knowledge of a nation without a constitution. Wherever Europeans have penetrated they have found some form of State organization, rude though it may have been. This recognition of the primordial character of the State is very widespread at the present day, but was in fact discovered in the eighteenth century. Eichhorn, Niebuhr, and Savigny were the first to show that the State is the constituted people. It was indeed a familiar fact to the Ancients in their great and simple Age. For them the State was a divinely appointed order, the origins of which were not subject to inquiry.

* * *

If, then, political capacity is innate in man, and is to be further developed, it is quite inaccurate to call the State a necessary evil. We have to deal with it as a lofty necessity of Nature. Even as the possibility of building up a civilization is dependent upon the limitation of our powers combined with the gift of reason, so also the State depends upon our inability to live alone. This Aristotle has already demonstrated. The State, says he, arose in order to make life possible; it endured to make good life possible.

* * *

Ultramontanes and Jacobins both start with the assumption that the legislation of a modern State is the work of sinful man. They thus display their total lack of reverence for the objectively revealed Will of God, as unfolded in the life of the State.

* * *

. . . if we simply look upon the State as intended to secure life and property to the individual, how comes it that the individual will also sacrifice life and property to the State? It is a false conclusion that wars are waged for the sake of material advantage. Modern wars are not fought for the sake of booty. Here the high moral ideal of national honour is a factor handed down from one generation to another, enshrining something positively sacred, and compelling the individual to sacrifice himself to it. This ideal is above all price and cannot be reduced to pounds, shillings, and pence. Kant says, "Where a price can be paid, an equivalent can be substituted. It is that which is above price and which consequently admits of no equivalent, that possesses real value." Genuine patriotism is the consciousness of co-operating with the body-politic, of being rooted in ancestral achievements and of transmitting them to descendants. Fichte has finely said, "Individual man sees in his country the realisation of his earthly immortality."

This involves that the State has a personality, primarily in the juridical, and secondly in the politico-moral sense.

* * *

Treat the State as a person, and the necessary and rational multiplicity of States follows. Just as in individual life the ego implies the existence of the non-ego, so it does in the State. The State is power, precisely in order to assert itself as against other equally independent powers. War and the administration of justice are the chief tasks of even the most barbaric States. But these tasks are only conceivable where a plurality of States are found existing side by side. Thus the idea of one universal empire is odious—the ideal of a State co-extensive with humanity is no ideal at all. In a single State the whole range of culture could never be fully spanned; no single people could unite the virtues of aristocracy and democracy. All nations, like all individuals, have their limitations, but it is exactly in the abundance of these limited qualities that the genius of humanity is exhibited. The rays of the Divine light are manifested, broken by countless facets among the separate peoples, each one exhibiting another picture and another idea of the whole. Every people has a right to believe that certain attributes of the Divine reason are exhibited in it to their fullest perfection. . . .

The features of history are virile, unsuited to sentimental or feminine natures. Brave peoples alone have an existence, an evolution or a future; the weak and cowardly perish, and perish justly. The grandeur of history lies in the perpetual conflict of nations, and it is simply foolish to desire the suppression of their rivalry. Mankind has ever found it to be so. The Kingdoms of the Diadochi and the hellenized nations of the East were the natural reaction from the world-empire of Alexander. The extreme one-sidedness of the idea of nationality which has been formed during our century by countries big and small is nothing but the natural revulsion against the world-empire of Napoleon. The unhappy attempt to transform the multiplicity of European life into the arid uniformity of universal sovereignty has produced the exclusive sway of nationality as the dominant political idea. Cosmopolitanism has receded too far.

These examples show clearly that there is no prospect of a settlement of international contradictions. The civilization of nations as well as of individuals tends to specialization. The subtleties of personal character assert themselves proportionately to increase of culture, and with its growth even the differences between nations become more sharply defined. In spite of the increased facilities of communications between different countries, no blending of their peculiarities has taken place; on the contrary, the more delicate distinctions of national character are far more marked to-day than in the Middle Ages. . . .

Further, if we examine our definition of the State as "the people legally united as an independent entity," we find that it can be more briefly put thus: "The State is the public force for Offence and Defence." It is, above all, Power which makes its will to prevail, it is not the totality of the people as Hegel assumes in his deification of it. The nation is not entirely comprised in the State, but the State protects and embraces the people's life, regulating its external aspects on every side. It does not ask primarily for opinion, but demands obedience, and its laws must be obeyed, whether willingly or no. . . .

The State is not an Academy of Arts. If it neglects its strength in order to promote the idealistic aspirations of man, it repudiates its own nature and perishes. This is in truth for the State equivalent to the sin against the Holy Ghost, for it is indeed a mortal error in the State to subordinate itself for sentimental reasons to a foreign Power, as we Germans have often done to England.

We have described the State as an independent force. This pregnant theory of independence implies firstly so absolute a moral supremacy that the State cannot legitimately tolerate any power above its own, and secondly a temporal freedom entailing a variety of material resources adequate to its protection against hostile influences. Legal sovereignty, the State's complete independence of any other earthly power, is so rooted in its nature that it may be said to be its very standard and criterion. . . .

The notion of sovereignty must not be rigid, but flexible and relative, like all political conceptions. Every State, in treaty making, will limit its power in certain directions for its own sake. States which conclude treaties with each other thereby curtail their absolute authority to some extent. But the rule still stands, for every treaty is a voluntary curb upon the power of each, and all international agreements are prefaced by the clause "Rebus sic stantibus." No State can pledge its future to another. It knows no arbiter, and draws up all its treaties with this implied reservation. This is supported by the axiom that so long as international law exists all treaties lose their force at the very moment when war is declared between the contracting parties; moreover, every sovereign State has the undoubted right to declare war at its pleasure, and is consequently entitled to repudiate its treaties. Upon this constantly recurring alteration of treaties the progress of history depends; every State must take care that its treaties do not survive their effective value, lest another Power should denounce them by a declaration of war; for antiquated treaties must necessarily be denounced and replaced by others more consonant with circumstances.

It is clear that the international agreements which limit the power of a State are not absolute, but voluntary self-restrictions. Hence, it follows that the establishment of a permanent international Arbitration Court is incompatible with the nature of the State, which could at all events only accept the decision of such a tribunal in cases of second- or third-rate importance. When a nation's existence is at stake there is no outside Power whose impartiality can be trusted.

* * *

If we apply the test of "autarchy" we perceive that, as Europe is now constituted, the larger States are constantly gaining influence in proportion as our international system assumes a more and more aristocratic complexion. The time is not yet very distant when the adhesion or withdrawal of such States as Piedmont and Savoy could actually decide the fate of a coalition. Today such a thing would be impossible. Since the Seven Years' War the domination of the five great Powers has been necessarily evolved. The big European questions are decided within this circle. Italy is on the verge of being admitted into it, but neither Belgium, Sweden, nor Switzerland have a voice unless their interests are directly concerned.

The entire development of European polity tends unmistakeably to drive the second-rate Powers into the background. . . .

On close examination then, it becomes clear that if the State is power, only that State which has power realizes its own idea, and this accounts for the undeniably ridiculous element which we discern in the existence of a small State. Weakness is not itself ridiculous, except when masquerading as strength.

* * *

When we begin to consider the aim of the State we are immediately confronted with the old vexed question which has needlessly fretted both the learned and the ignorant, namely—Should we look upon it as a means towards the private ends for which its citizens strive, or are those citizens means towards the great national ends of the State? The severely political outlook of the ancient world favoured the second alternative; the first is maintained by the modern social conception of the State, and the eighteenth century believed itself to have discovered in it the theory that the State should be treated only as an instrument to promote the aims of its citizens.

But, as Falstaff would say, this is "a question not to be asked," for ever since it has been considered at all, it has been universally agreed that the rights and duties of the State and its members are reciprocal. There can be no two opinions on that point. But parties which are bound together by mutual obligations and rights cannot stand to each other in the relations of means to an end, for means only exist to serve an end, and there can be no reciprocity between them. The Christian point of view has destroyed the ancient conception of the State, and the Christian would be false to himself if he did not reserve that immortal and intransitory something, which we call conscience, as his own private and peculiar possession.

In one of his greatest books, *The Foundations of the Metaphysics of Ethics,* Kant logically develops the principle that no human being may be used merely as an instrument, thereby recognizing the divinely appointed dignity of man. Conversely, to regard the State as nothing but a means for the citizens' ends is to place the subjective aspect too high. The greatness of the State lies precisely in its power of uniting the past with the present and the future; and consequently no individual has the right to regard the State as the servant of his own aims but is bound by moral duty and physical necessity to subordinate himself to it, while the State lies under the obligation to concern itself with the life of its citizens by extending to them its help and protection.

* * *

The next essential function of the State is the conduct of war. The long oblivion into which this principle had fallen is a proof of how effeminate the science of government had become in civilian hands. In our century this sentimentality was dissipated by Clausewitz, but a one-sided materialism arose in its place, after the fashion of the Manchester school, seeing in man a biped creature, whose destiny lies in buying cheap and selling dear. It is obvious that this idea is not compatible with war, and it is only since the last war that a sounder theory arose of the State and its military power.

Without war no State could be. All those we know of arose through war, and the protection of their members by armed force remains their primary and essential task. War, therefore, will endure to the end of history, as long as there is multiplicity of States. The laws of human thought and of human nature forbid any alternative, neither is one to be wished for. The blind worshipper of an eternal peace falls into the error of isolating the State, or dreams of one which is universal, which we have already seen to be at variance with reason.

Even as it is impossible to conceive of a tribunal above the State, which we have recognized as sovereign in its very essence, so it is likewise impossible to banish the idea of war from the world. It is a favourite fashion of our time to instance England as particularly ready for peace. But England is perpetually at war; there is hardly an instant in her recent history in which she has not been obliged to be fighting somewhere. The great strides which civilization makes against barbarism and unreason are only made actual by the sword. Between civilized nations also war is the form of litigation by which States make their claims valid. The arguments brought forward in these terrible law suits of the nations compel as no argument in civil suits can ever do. Often as we have tried by theory to convince the small States that Prussia alone can be the leader in Germany, we had to produce the final proof upon the battlefields of Bohemia and the Main.

Moreover war is a uniting as well as a dividing element among nations; it does not draw them together in enmity only, for through its means they learn to know and to respect each other's peculiar qualities. . . .

The grandeur of war lies in the utter annihilation of puny man in the great conception of the State, and it brings out the full magnificence of the sacrifice of fellow-countrymen for one another. In war the chaff is winnowed from the wheat. Those who have lived through 1870 cannot fail to understand Niebuhr's description of his feelings in 1813, when he speaks of how no one who has entered into the joy of being bound by a common tie to all his compatriots, gentle and simple alike, can ever forget how he was uplifted by the love, the friendliness, and the strength of that mutual sentiment.

It is war which fosters the political idealism which the materialist rejects. What a disaster for civilization it would be if mankind blotted its heroes from memory. The heroes of a nation are the figures which rejoice and inspire the spirit of its youth, and the writers whose words ring like trumpet blasts become the idols of our boyhood and our early manhood. He who feels no answering thrill is unworthy to bear arms for his country.

Imperialism, the Latest Stage of Capitalism

V.I. Lenin

These are excerpts from a lengthy polemical pamphlet that Lenin wrote in 1916. For ideological reasons, the work was later renamed Imperialism, the Highest Stage of Capitalism, *the title by which it is commonly known today.*

The export of *goods* was characteristic of the old capitalism, under the complete control of free competition. For the new capitalism, controlled by monopoly, the export of *capital* has become characteristic . . .

Of course if capitalism could develop agriculture, which today has everywhere fallen terribly far behind industry, if it could raise the standard of living of the bulk of the population, who everywhere remain, despite dizzying technological progress, half-starved and impoverished—then there could be no talk of a capital surplus. And this is the argument usually advanced by *petit-bourgeois* critics of capitalism.[1] But then capitalism would not be capitalism, for both unevenness of development and semi-starvation living standards are fundamental, inevitable conditions and prerequisites of this mode of production. As long as capitalism remains capitalism, a surplus of capital will be deployed not to raise the general standard of living in a given country—since this would lower the profits of the capitalists—but to raise profits by exporting capital abroad to the backward countries. In these backward countries profits are usually high, because there is little capital, the price of land is comparatively low, wages are low, and raw materials are cheap. It is *possible* to export capital because a number of backward countries have already been drawn into the world capitalist economic system, major railway lines have been built or are under construction, the elementary conditions for industrial development have been secured, and so on. It is *necessary* to export capital because in several countries capitalism has become "over-ripe," and capital has no field for profitable investment, given the underdevelopment of agriculture and the poverty of the masses . . .

The export of capital influences the development of capitalism, greatly accelerating it in the countries to which it is directed. If therefore, to some extent, this export can lead to stagnation in the development of the exporting countries, this can happen only at the price of permitting an intensification of the further development of capitalism throughout the world . . .

[T]he defining characteristic of the period we are examining is the final partitioning of the world, final not in the sense that it cannot be *repartitioned*—repartition is possible, even inevitable—but in the sense that the colonial policy of the capitalist countries has *completed* the seizure of the unoccupied land on our planet. The world, for the first time, is completely partitioned, so henceforth there can be *only* repartition, that is, transfer from one "proprietor" to another, rather than from an ownerless to an "owned" state.

Thus we are living in a distinctive era of global colonial policy, which is very closely connected to the "latest stage in the development of capitalism"—finance capital . . .

It is not only the already-discovered sources of raw materials that are of interest to finance capital, but also potential sources, for technology is developing with incredible speed in our era, and land that is useless today can perhaps be made useful tomorrow if new methods are found (to this end a major bank can mount a special expedition of engineers, agronomists, etc.) and if a large expenditure of capital is made. The same principle applies to prospecting for mineral wealth, new methods of processing and utilizing raw materials, and so on. Hence the inevitable aspiration of finance capital to increase its territory. Just as the trusts capitalize their holdings at two or three times their value, taking into account "potential" profits in the future (and not just in the present) and subsequent results of monopoly, in general finance capital strives to capture as much land as it can, wherever and however it can, taking into account possible sources of raw materials, afraid of falling behind in the mad scramble for the last morsels of the unpartitioned world, or for the repartition of morsels already divided up.

. . . . . .

We must now try to summarize what we know, to gather together what has been said above about imperialism. Imperialism arose as a development of the fundamental characteristics of capitalism in general. But capitalism became capitalist imperialism only at a particular, very high stage of its development, when some of the fundamental characteristics of capitalism began to turn into their opposites, when the characteristics of the era of transition from capitalism to a higher socio-economic structure had taken form and revealed themselves. Economically, the most important thing was a change from capitalist free competition to capitalist monopoly.

Free competition is the essential characteristic of capitalism, and of commodity production in general; monopoly is the exact opposite of free competition, but the latter has transformed itself into monopoly before our very eyes, creating large-scale industry and forcing out the small, replacing the large with the even larger, pushing the concentration of industry and capital to the point where out of it has arisen and is arising monopoly:—cartels, syndicates, trusts—merging with the capital of the ten or so banks that control billions. At the same time the monopolies, which have arisen out of free competition, do not eliminate it but exist above and beside it, thus engendering a series of particularly acute and abrupt contradictions, clashes, and conflicts. Monopoly is the transition from capitalism to a higher system.

If we had to give the shortest possible definition of imperialism, we would therefore have to say that imperialism is the monopolistic phase of capitalism. This definition would capture the most important point for, on the one hand, the finance capital of a few enormous monopolistic banks has merged with the capital of the monopolist cartels of industrialists; and on the other hand, the partition of the world is a transition from a colonial policy that has freely extended to all territories as yet unseized by a capitalist power, to a colonial policy of monopolist possession of all the world's land, carried through to the end.

But excessively short definitions, useful as they are to sum up the most important points, are nonetheless insufficient, because we need to deduce from them the particularly essential features of the phenomenon that we must define. Therefore, without forgetting the conventional and relative significance of definitions—which can never encompass completely all the multitudinous features of a phenomenon in its full development—we must provide a definition of imperialism that includes the following five fundamental features: (1) the concentration of production and capital has reached such a high stage that it has produced monopolies which play a decisive role in economic life; (2) the merging of bank capital with industrial capital, creating on the basis of this "finance capital" a financial oligarchy; (3) the export of capital, as opposed to the export of goods, acquires a particularly important significance; (4) the formation of international monopolistic alliances of capitalists, dividing up the world among themselves; and (5) the completion of the territorial division of the globe by the major capitalist powers. Imperialism is capitalism at that stage of development when the dominance of monopoly and financial capital has been established, the export of capital has acquired outstanding importance, the division of the world by international trusts has begun, and the partition of all the earth's territories by the major capitalist countries has been completed.

. . . . . .

As we have seen, the deepest economic foundation of imperialism is monopoly. This is capitalist monopoly, *i.e.* monopoly that has arisen out of capitalism and exists in the general environment of capitalism—commodity production and competition—in permanent and irresolvable contradiction to this environment. Nevertheless, like all monopoly it inevitably creates a tendency toward stagnation and decay. Because monopoly prices are fixed, if only temporarily, to some extent incentives for technological—and consequently for all other—progress disappear. Furthermore, there arises the *economic* possibility that technological progress will be deliberately retarded. For example, in America a man named Owens invented a bottle-making machine that revolutionized the manufacture of bottles. The German cartel of bottle manufacturers bought the Owens patents and set them aside rather than use them. Of course, under capitalism monopoly can never totally and permanently eliminate competition in the global market . . . And of course the possibility of lowering production costs and raising profits by means of technological improvements is an impetus toward change. But the *tendency* toward stagnation and decay that is characteristic of monopoly will continue to operate, and in certain branches of industry, in certain countries, in certain periods of time, it will prevail.

Monopolist possession of particularly vast, rich, or conveniently located colonies will work in the same way.

Further, imperialism is an enormous accumulation of money capital in a handful of countries, reaching, as we have seen, the level of 100–150 million francs in securities. Hence the extraordinary growth of a class or, more accurately, a stratum of *rentiers, i.e.* people who live by "clipping coupons"—people entirely disconnected from participation in any kind of enterprise—people whose profession is idleness. The export of capital, one of the most essential foundations of imperialism, further intensifies this complete isolation of the *rentier* stratum from production and marks as parasitic the entire country that lives by exploiting the labor of several overseas countries and colonies.

. . . . . .

On the one hand the enormous amount of finance capital concentrated in a few hands, creating an extraordinarily extensive and dense network of relationships and connections that subordinates not only all of the medium-sized and small but even the very small capitalists and proprietors; on the other hand, the intensifying struggle against groups of financiers in the other nation-states for the partition of the world and domination over other lands—together these have brought about the unanimous conversion of the propertied classes to the imperialist cause. "Universal" enthusiasm about the prospects for imperialism, rabid defense of it, portraying it as attractively as possible—these are the signs of the times. Imperialist ideology even cozies up to the working class. There is no Chinese wall separating it from the other classes.[2] The leaders of today's so-called "Social Democratic" party in Germany[3] have truly earned the designation "social imperialist," *i.e.* socialists in word but imperialists in deed, while in 1902 Hobson had already noted the existence of "Fabian imperialists" in England, members of the opportunistic Fabian Society.[4]

. . . . . .

We have seen how the economic essence of imperialism is monopoly capitalism. This is what defines its place in history, for monopoly that develops in the context of free competition, to be exact *out of* free competition, is the transition from capitalism to a higher socio-economic structure. We must note in particular four principal aspects of monopoly, or principal manifestations of monopoly capitalism, that characterize the era we are examining.

First, monopoly arose out of the concentration of production at a very high stage of its development. This means monopolist associations of capitalists, cartels, syndicates, and trusts. We have seen what an enormous role they play in contemporary economic life. By the beginning of the 20th century they had achieved total supremacy in the advanced countries. Although the first steps toward forming cartels had been taken earlier by countries with high protective tariffs (Germany, America),

Great Britain, with her system of free trade, only slightly later displayed the same basic reality: the birth of monopoly out of the concentration of production.

Second, monopolies have accelerated the seizure of the most important sources of raw materials, especially for the basic and most highly cartelized industries of capitalist society: coal-mining and iron-making. Monopolistic control of the most important sources of raw materials has greatly increased the power of giant capital and intensified the antagonism between cartelized and non-cartelized industry.

Third, monopoly was an outgrowth of the banks. They have transformed themselves from modest intermediary enterprises into monopolists of finance capital. Some three to five enormous banks in each of the leading capitalist countries have accomplished the "intimate union" of industrial and finance capital; they have concentrated in their hands control of countless millions, constituting the greater part of the capital and monetary income of the entire nation. A financial oligarchy that imposes a dense network of relationships of dependency on absolutely all of the economic and political institutions of contemporary bourgeois society—this is the most striking manifestation of this monopoly.

Fourth, monopoly is an outgrowth of colonial policy. To the many "old" motives of colonial policy, finance capital has added a struggle for sources of raw materials, for the export of capital, for "spheres of influence"—*i.e.* zones for advantageous deals, concessions, monopolistic profits, *etc.*—in the end for economic territory in general. For example, when European colonial holdings comprised only 10% of Africa, as was the case in 1876, colonial policy could develop by non-monopolistic means—"free seizure" of territory, so to speak. But when, by 1900, 90% of Africa had been seized, when the whole world had been partitioned, inevitably the era of monopoly possession of colonies and, consequently, of particularly intense competition for the division and re-division of the world, began.

The extent to which monopoly capitalism has intensified all the contradictions of capitalism is well known. It will suffice to point out the high cost of living and the yoke of the cartels. This intensification of contradictions is the most powerful motive force of the transitional historical period that began with the conclusive victory of international finance capital.

Monopolies, oligarchies, a struggle for supremacy rather than for freedom, exploitation of an ever larger number of small or weak countries by a handful of wealthy or powerful nations[5]—all of this has engendered the distinguishing characteristics of imperialism which compel us to define it as parasitic or decaying capitalism. More and more conspicuously the creation of the "rentier state," the money-lender state, whose bourgeoisie increasingly lives off the export of capital and "clipping coupons," emerges as one of the tendencies of imperialism. It would be a mistake to think that this tendency toward decay precludes rapid growth of capitalism. On the contrary, in the era of imperialism certain branches of industry, certain strata of the bourgeoisie, and certain countries display, to a greater or lesser extent, now one, now another of these tendencies. Overall, capitalism is growing immeasurably faster than before. However, not only is this growth becoming more and more uneven in general, but the unevenness is particularly evident in the decay of the countries strongest in capital (Britain) . . .

In its turn, this extraordinarily fast-growing finance capital, precisely because it has grown so quickly, doesn't mind moving along to a "quieter" possession of colonies subject to seizure—and not by peaceful means alone—from richer countries. For the last few decades, economic development has proceeded even faster in the United States than in Germany; it is precisely *because* of this that the parasitic characteristics of the new American capitalism are so clearly evident. On the other hand, if you were to compare the republican American bourgeoisie with the monarchist bourgeoisie of Japan or Germany, you would see that enormous political differences weaken considerably in the era of imperialism—not because they are not important in general, but because in all of these instances we are talking about a bourgeoisie with the characteristic features of parasitism.

Receipt of high monopolistic profits by the capitalists in one of the many branches of industry, in one of the many countries, *etc.,* gives them the economic means to buy off certain strata of the workers—and for a while at least a significant minority of them—bringing them over to the side of a given industry or a given nation against all others. And the intensifying antagonism among the imperialist nations for the partition of the world strengthens this effort. This is the basis for the bond between imperialism and opportunism[6] that was evident earliest and most clearly in Britain, due to the fact that certain features of imperialist development were evident there much earlier than in other countries . . . In fact the extraordinary rapidity and loathsomeness of the development of opportunism do not guarantee its enduring success; the rapid growth of a malignant boil on a healthy organism can only hasten the boil's bursting, freeing the organism from it. Most dangerous of all in this respect are people who do not want to understand that the struggle against imperialism is an empty and dishonest phrase unless it is inseparably joined with the struggle against opportunism . . .

Notes

1. The phrase "*petit-bourgeois*" functions as a term of general-purpose abuse in the writings of early twentieth-century Communists. Strictly speaking it means "from the lower ranks of the bourgeoisie," but as commonly used it is not necessarily an accurate description of the class origins of the person or persons being denounced. Here as elsewhere, it can best be understood as meaning "people who think they are on the Left because they criticize capitalism, but who are actually capitalist dupes because they don't read enough Marx and/or don't interpret him the same way I do."

2. Lenin is referring, metaphorically, to the Great Wall of China.

3. The Social Democratic Party (SPD) was Germany's largest mass political party. Backed by the labor unions, it was a socialist party, but Lenin considered the SPD insufficiently Marxist and insufficiently critical of German imperialism.

4. The Fabian Society was a small but influential group of British socialists led by Sidney and Beatrice Webb. For a variety of reasons too complicated to explain here, they actively supported continued expansion of the British Empire.

5. When Lenin says "small or weak," he is probably thinking not only of small Third World territories but also of China, which though vast and populous was also subject to commercial exploitation by the imperial powers because of its military weakness. When he says "wealthy or powerful," he is undoubtedly thinking not only of wealthy capitalist nations like Britain and France but also of his own country, Russia, which had just begun to industrialize and had little capital, but which had amassed considerable territory on its borders through military force.

6. Lenin considered support for imperialism by the leaders of a socialist party unprincipled. He uses the word "opportunism" here because he assumes that these leaders must be driven by unworthy motives: they are trying to curry favor with their national elites and/or trying to attract votes from their jingoistic countrymen. The possibility that they might be sincere, if perhaps mistaken, he does not consider.

Translated from the Russian and annotated by Kathleen Callanan Martin

Confession of Faith

Cecil Rhodes

Rhodes originally wrote this on June 2, 1877, in Oxford. Later, that year in Kimberley, he made some additions and changes. What follows is that amended statement. The spelling and grammar errors were in the original.

It often strikes a man to inquire what is the chief good in life; to one the thought comes that it is a happy marriage, to another great wealth, and as each seizes on his idea, for that he more or less works for the rest of his existence. To myself thinking over the same question the wish came to render myself useful to my country. I then asked myself how could I and after reviewing the various methods I have felt that at the present day we are actually limiting our children and perhaps bringing into the world half the human beings we might owing to the lack of country for them to inhabit that if we had retained America there would at this moment be millions more of English living. **I contend that we are the finest race in the world and that the more of the world we inhabit the better it is for the human race. Just fancy those parts that are at present inhabited by the most despicable specimens of human beings what an alteration there would be if they were brought under Anglo-Saxon influence, look again at the extra employment a new country added to our dominions gives.** I contend that every acre added to our territory means in the future birth to some more of the English race who otherwise would not be brought into existence. Added to this the absorption of the greater portion of the world under our rule simply means the end of all wars, at this moment had we not lost America I believe we could have stopped the Russian-Turkish war by merely refusing money and supplies. Having these ideas what scheme could we think of to forward this object. **I look into history and I read the story of the Jesuits I see what they were able to do in a bad cause and I might say under bad leaders.**

At the present day I become a member of the Masonic order I see the wealth and power they possess the influence they hold and I think over their ceremonies and I wonder that a large body of men can devote themselves to what at times appear the most ridiculous and absurd rites without an object and without an end.

The idea gleaming and dancing before ones eyes like a will-of-the-wisp at last frames itself into a plan. **Why should we not form a secret society with but one**

object the furtherance of the British Empire and the bringing of the whole unci-vilised world under British rule for the recovery of the United States for the making the Anglo-Saxon race but one Empire. What a dream, but yet it is probable, it is possible. I once heard it argued by a fellow in my own college, I am sorry to own it by an Englishman, that it was good thing for us that we have lost the United States. There are some subjects on which there can be no arguments, and to an Englishman this is one of them, but <u>even from an American's point of view just picture what they have lost</u>, look at their government, are not the frauds that yearly come before the public view a disgrace to any country and especially their's which is the finest in the world. Would they have occurred had they remained under English rule great as they have become how infinitely greater they would have been with the softening and elevating influences of English rule, think of those countless 000's of Englishmen that during the last 100 years would have crossed the Atlantic and settled and populated the United States. Would they have not made without any prejudice a finer country of it than the low class Irish and German emigrants? All this we have lost and that country loses owing to whom? Owing to two or three ignorant pig-headed statesmen of the last century, at their door lies the blame. Do you ever feel mad? do you ever feel murderous. I think I do with those men. I bring facts to prove my assertion. Does an English father when his sons wish to emigrate ever think of suggesting emigration to a country under another flag, never—it would seem a disgrace to suggest such a thing I think that we all think that poverty is better under our own flag than wealth under a foreign one.

Put your mind into another train of thought. Fancy Australia discovered and colonised under the French flag, what would it mean merely several millions of English unborn that at present exist we learn from the past and to form our future. We learn from having lost to cling to what we possess. We know the size of the world we know the total extent. **Africa is still lying ready for us it is our duty to take it. It is our duty to seize every opportunity of acquiring more territory and we should keep this one idea steadily before our eyes that more territory simply means more of the Anglo-Saxon race more of the best the most human, most honourable race the world possesses.**

To forward such a scheme what a splendid help a secret society would be a society not openly acknowledged but who would work in secret for such an object.

I contend that there are at the present moment numbers of the ablest men in the world who would devote their whole lives to it. I often think what a loss to the English nation in some respects the abolition of the Rotten Borough System has been. What thought strikes a man entering the house of commons, the assembly that rule the whole world? I think it is the mediocrity of the men but what is the cause. It is simply—an assembly of wealth of men whose lives have been spent in the accumulation of money and whose time has been too much engaged to be able to spare any for the study of past history. And yet in hands of such men rest our destinies. Do men like the great Pitt, and Burke and Sheridan not now to exist. I contend they do. There are men now living with I know no other term the [Greek term] of Aristotle but there are not ways for enabling them to serve their Country. They live and die unused unemployed. What has the main cause of the success of the Romish Church? The fact that every enthusiast, call it if you like every madman finds employment in it. **Let us form the same kind of society a Church for the extension of the British**

Empire. **A society which should have members in every part of the British Empire working with one object and one idea we should have its members placed at our universities and our schools and should watch the English youth passing through their hands just one perhaps in every thousand would have the mind and feelings for such an object, he should be tried in every way, he should be tested whether he is endurant, possessed of eloquence, disregardful of the petty details of life, and if found to be such, then elected and bound by oath to serve for the rest of his life in his County.** He should then be supported if without means by the Society and sent to that part of the Empire where it was felt he was needed.

Take another case, let us fancy a man who finds himself his own master with ample means of attaining his majority whether he puts the question directly to himself or not, still like the old story of virtue and vice in the Memorabilia a fight goes on in him as to what he should do. Take if he plunges into dissipation there is nothing too reckless he does not attempt but after a time his life palls on him, he mentally says this is not good enough, he changes his life, he reforms, he travels, he thinks now I have found the chief good in life, the novelty wears off, and he tires, to change again, he goes into the far interior after the wild game he thinks at last I've found that in life of which I cannot tire, again he is disappointed. He returns he thinks is there nothing I can do in life? Here I am with means, with a good house, with everything that is to be envied and yet I am not happy I am tired of life he possesses within him a portion of the [Greek term] of Aristotle but he knows it not, to such a man the Society should go, should test, and should finally show him the greatness of the scheme and list him as a member.

Take one more case of the younger son with high thoughts, high aspirations, endowed by nature with all the faculties to make a great man, and with the sole wish in life to serve his Country but he lacks two things the means and the opportunity, ever troubled by a sort of inward deity urging him on to high and noble deeds, he is compelled to pass his time in some occupation which furnishes him with mere existence, he lives unhappily and dies miserably. Such men as these the Society should search out and use for the furtherance of their object.

(In every Colonial legislature the Society should attempt to have its members prepared at all times to vote or speak and advocate the closer union of England and the colonies, to crush all disloyalty and every movement for the severance of our Empire. The Society should inspire and even own portions of the press for the press rules the mind of the people. The Society should always be searching for members who might by their position in the world by their energies or character forward the object but the ballot and test for admittance should be severe)

Once make it common and it fails. Take a man of great wealth who is bereft of his children perhaps having his mind soured by some bitter disappointment who shuts himself up separate from his neighbours and makes up his mind to a miserable existence. To such men as these the society should go gradually disclose the greatness of their scheme and entreat him to throw in his life and property with them for this object. I think that there are thousands now existing who would eagerly grasp at the opportunity. Such are the heads of my scheme.

For fear that death might cut me off before the time for attempting its development I leave all my worldly goods in trust to S. G. Shippard and the Secretary for the Colonies at the time of my death to try to form such a Society with such an object.

On September 19, 1877, Rhodes drafted his first will; at that time, he had an estate of only about £10,000. (Although he changed his will quite a number of times in years following, the objective remained the same. After his death, the directors of the Rhodes Trust set up the Rhodes Scholarships as the best way to achieve his objectives.) The first clause of the 1877 will bequeathed his wealth as follows:

To and for the establishment, promotion and development of a Secret Society, the true aim and object whereof shall be for the extension of British rule throughout the world, the perfecting of a system of emigration from the United Kingdom, and of colonisation by British subjects of all lands where the means of livelihood are attainable by energy, labour and enterprise, and especially the occupation by British settlers of the entire Continent of Africa, the Holy Land, the Valley of the Euphrates, the Islands of Cyprus and Candia, the whole of South America, the Islands of the Pacific not heretofore possessed by Great Britain, the whole of the Malay Archipelago, the seaboard of China and Japan, the ultimate recovery of the United States of America as an integral part of the British Empire, the inauguration of a system of Colonial representation in the Imperial Parliament which may tend to weld together the disjointed members of the Empire and, finally, the foundation of so great a Power as to render wars impossible and promote the best interests of humanity.

On the Democratic Welfare State

Franklin D. Roosevelt

Franklin D. Roosevelt was born in 1882 at Hyde Park, N.Y. He was edu-cated at Groton, Harvard, and the Columbia Law School. He served as Assistant Secretary of the Navy, 1913–1920. In 1921 he suffered a severe attack of infantile paralysis, but in subsequent years he recovered the par-tial use of his legs. He was governor of New York, 1929–1933, and President of the United States from 1933 until his death on April 12, 1945.

His second inaugural address on January 20, 1937, surveyed the achievements of his first term and the problems requiring further action. It is presented as an expression of the New Deal philosophy of democracy.

This address has been reprinted in various volumes, including The Public Papers and Addresses of Franklin D. Roosevelt, 1937 Volume, *New York, The Macmillan Company, 1941.*

When four years ago we met to inaugurate a President, the Republic, single-minded in anxiety, stood in spirit here. We dedicated ourselves to the fulfillment of a vision—to speed the time when there would be for all the people that security and peace essential to the pursuit of happiness. We of the Republic pledged ourselves to drive from the temple of our ancient faith those who had profaned it; to end by action, tireless and unafraid, the stagnation and despair of that day. We did those first things first.

Our covenant with ourselves did not stop there. Instinctively we recognized a deeper need—the need to find through government the instrument of our united purpose to solve for the individual the ever-rising problems of a complex civilization. Repeated attempts at their solution without the aid of government had left us baffled and bewildered. For, without that aid, we had been unable to create those moral con-trols over the services of science which are necessary to make science a useful servant instead of a ruthless master of mankind. To do this we knew that we must find prac-tical controls over blind economic forces and blindly selfish men.

We of the Republic sensed the truth that democratic government has innate capacity to protect its people against disasters once considered inevitable, to solve problems once considered unsolvable. We would not admit that we could not find a way to master economic epidemics just as, after centuries of fatalistic suffering, we had found a way to master epidemics of disease. We refused to leave the problems of our common welfare to be solved by the winds of chance and the hurricanes of disaster.

In this we Americans were discovering no wholly new truth; we were writing a new chapter in our book of self-government.

This year marks the one hundred and fiftieth anniversary of the Constitutional Convention which made us a nation. At that Convention our forefathers found the way out of the chaos which followed the Revolutionary War; they created a strong government with powers of united action sufficient then and now to solve problems utterly beyond individual or local solution. A century and a half ago they established the Federal Government in order to promote the general welfare and secure the blessings of liberty to the American people.

Today we invoke those same powers of government to achieve the same objectives.

Four years of new experience have not belied our historic instinct. They hold out the clear hope that government within communities, government within the separate States, and government of the United States can do the things the times require, without yielding its democracy. Our tasks in the last four years did not force democracy to take a holiday.

Nearly all of us recognize that as intricacies of human relationships increase, so power to govern them also must increase—power to stop evil; power to do good. The essential democracy of our Nation and the safety of our people depend not upon the absence of power, but upon lodging it with those whom the people can change or continue at stated intervals through an honest and free system of elections. The Constitution of 1787 did not make our democracy impotent.

In fact, in these last four years, we have made the exercise of all power more democratic; for we have begun to bring private autocratic powers into their proper subordination to the public's government. The legend that they were invincible— above and beyond the processes of a democracy—has been shattered. They have been challenged and beaten.

Our progress out of the depression is obvious. But that is not all that you and I mean by the new order of things. Our pledge was not merely to do a patchwork job with second-hand materials. By using the new materials of social justice we have undertaken to erect on the old foundations a more enduring structure for the better use of future generations.

In that purpose we have been helped by achievements of mind and spirit. Old truths have been relearned; untruths have been unlearned. We have always known that heedless self-interest was bad morals; we know now that it is bad economics. Out of the collapse of a prosperity whose builders boasted their practicality has come the conviction that in the long run economic morality pays. We are beginning to wipe out the line that divides the practical from the ideal; and in so doing we are fashioning an instrument of unimagined power for the establishment of a morally better world.

This new understanding undermines the old admiration of worldly success as such. We are beginning to abandon our tolerance of the abuse of power by those who betray for profit the elementary decencies of life.

In this process evil things formerly accepted will not be so easily condoned. Hardheadedness will not so easily excuse hard-heartedness. We are moving toward an era of good feeling. But we realize that there can be no era of good feeling save among men of goodwill.

For these reasons I am justified in believing that the greatest change we have witnessed has been the change in the moral climate of America.

Among men of goodwill, science and democracy together offer an ever-richer life and ever-larger satisfaction to the individual. With this change in our moral climate and our rediscovered ability to improve our economic order, we have set our feet upon the road of enduring progress.

Shall we pause now and turn our back upon the road that lies ahead? Shall we call this the promised land? Or, shall we continue on our way? For "each age is a dream that is dying, or one that is coming to birth."

Many voices are heard as we face a great decision. Comfort says, "Tarry a while." Opportunism says, "This is a good spot." Timidity asks, "How difficult is the road ahead?"

True, we have come far from the days of stagnation and despair. Vitality has been preserved. Courage and confidence have been restored. Mental and moral horizons have been extended.

But our present gains were won under the pressure of more than ordinary circumstance. Advance became imperative under the goad of fear and suffering. The times were on the side of progress.

To hold to progress today, however, is more difficult. Dulled conscience, irresponsibility, and ruthless self-interest already reappear. Such symptoms of prosperity may become portents of disaster! Prosperity already tests the persistence of our progressive purpose.

Let us ask again: Have we reached the goal of our vision of that fourth day of March, 1933? Have we found our happy valley?

I see a great nation, upon a great continent, blessed with a great wealth of natural resources. Its hundred and thirty million people are at peace among themselves; they are making their country a good neighbor among the nations. I see a United States which can demonstrate that, under democratic methods of government, national wealth can be translated into a spreading volume of human comforts hitherto unknown, and the lowest standard of living can be raised far above the level of mere subsistence.

But here is the challenge to our democracy: In this nation I see tens of millions of its citizens—a substantial part of its whole population—who at this very moment are denied the greater part of what the very lowest standards of today call the necessities of life.

I see millions of families trying to live on incomes so meager that the pall of family disaster hangs over them day by day.

I see millions whose daily lives in city and on farm continue under conditions labeled indecent by a so-called polite society half a century ago.

I see millions denied education, recreation, and the opportunity to better their lot and the lot of their children.

I see millions lacking the means to buy the products of farm and factory and by their poverty denying work and productiveness to many other millions.

I see one-third of a nation ill-housed, ill-clad, ill-nourished.

It is not in despair that I paint you that picture. I paint it for you in hope—because the Nation, seeing and understanding the injustice in it, proposes to paint it out. We are determined to make every American citizen the subject of his country's interest and concern; and we will never regard any faithful, law-abiding group within our borders as superfluous. The test of our progress is not whether we add more to the abundance of those who have much; it is whether we provide enough for those who have too little.

If I know aught of the spirit and purpose of our Nation, we will not listen to Comfort, Opportunism, and Timidity. We will carry on.

Overwhelmingly, we of the Republic are men and women of good will; men and women who have more than warm hearts of dedication; men and women who have cool heads and willing hands of practical purpose as well. They will insist that every agency of popular government use effective instruments to carry out their will.

Government is competent when all who compose it work as trustees for the whole people. It can make constant progress when it keeps abreast of all the facts. It can obtain justified support and legitimate criticism when the people receive true information of all that government does.

If I know aught of the will of the people, they will demand that these conditions of effective government shall be created and maintained. They will demand a Nation uncorrupted by cancers of injustice and, therefore, strong among the nations in its example of the will to peace.

Today we reconsecrate our country to long-cherished ideals in a suddenly changed civilization. In every land there are always at work forces that drive men apart and forces that draw men together. In our personal ambitions we are individualists. But in our seeking for economic and political progress as a nation, we all go up, or else we all go down, as one people.

To maintain a democracy of effort requires a vast amount of patience in dealing with different methods, a vast amount of humility. But out of the confusion of many voices rises an understanding of dominant public need. Then political leadership can voice common ideals, and aid in their realization.

In taking again the oath of office as President of the United States, I assume the solemn obligation of leading the American people forward along the road over which they have chosen to advance.

While this duty rests upon me I shall do my utmost to speak their purpose and to do their will, seeking Divine guidance to help us each and every one to give light to them that sit in darkness and to guide our feet into the way of peace.

For comparisons between democracy and other ideals, see Joseph A. Leighton, *Social Philosophies in Conflict: Fascism and Nazism, Communism, Liberal Democracy*, New York, Appleton-Century-Crofts, Inc., 1937; C. E. Merriam. *The New Democracy and the New Despotism*, New York, Whittlesey House, 1939; Kurt London. *Backgrounds of Conflict*, New York, The Macmillan Company, 1945.

The Social Bases of Nazism

David Schoenbaum

The rise of Nazism in Germany, and of similar movements in other countries, is the outstanding characteristic of the two decades between the world wars. How could such a movement take shape and win substantial support? Social scientists have developed a number of approaches in trying to deal with the phenomenon. Some see Nazism and other totalitarian movements as endemic in the condition of modern man. Robbed of traditional values, such as religion, and close community ties, modern man stands alone and fearful; he easily yields to the solidarity and discipline of movements such as Nazism. Others view Nazism as a specifically German phenomenon, seeking in the German past an acceptance of authority and militarism. Still others emphasize more temporary factors, maintaining that Nazism was the product of a massive and unexpected defeat in war and of a variety of severe economic pressures, all of which had much greater impact in Germany than elsewhere. Even amid unprecedented social and political stress Nazism did not really gain popularity until the Great Depression.

Interpretation of support for Nazism is further complicated by the sheer opportunism of the movement, which tried to appeal to almost all groups and was quite capable of switching stands to win support. Relatedly, the reasons Nazism won popularity differ considerably from the results of Nazism in practice. No one has yet clearly assessed the extent to which Nazi anti-Semitism and aggressive nationalism won support; all we know for sure is that they did not deter the Nazi voters. But Nazism's promises of support for small business and small farmers and its suggestion of a return to a more traditional Germany were directly contradicted by the actions of the regime once in power. It has even been argued that, horrible as it was, the Nazi movement ultimately helped make Germany more genuinely modern and thus less susceptible to similar movements—after Nazism itself was defeated in war.

The following selection seeks to explain the varied social bases of Nazism, dealing both with the immediate problems and the longer-range grievances that led people to embrace the movement. It emphasizes the persistence of anxieties about modernization. Were these anxieties, or at least the intensity with which they were experienced, peculiarly German? Are war and depression sufficient explanations for the way in which these anxieties were expressed? Questions like these must be faced, for in understanding Nazism's appeal we must try to estimate the chances of its recurrence, in Germany or elsewhere. This in turn leads us to ask what has happened to the social groups and values that supported Nazism. Have they changed or disappeared with further modernization? The passage stresses not only social but also generational tension during the period of Nazism's rise. Young people were disproportionately enthusiastic about the Nazi movement. Again we must try to determine whether this is because of peculiar circumstances in the period, or German characteristics, or perhaps more enduring problems of youth in modern society.

The concept of a sick society causes problems if only because no one knows exactly what constitutes social health. But to the extent that the concept has meaning, Germany after 1918 was an appropriate place for its application. The most spectacular symptoms—the propensity to physical violence, the hyperbolic inflation of 1923, and the near-overnight disintegration of the economy in 1929–30—had their equivalents elsewhere. But elsewhere they led to crises and convalescence recognizably within the limits of previous historical experience and the status quo. In Germany, however, the permanent disaffection of major social groups, the alienation of those groups who presumably support a liberal republic, was reflected in the progressive and total collapse of all liberal parties, and in the discrepancy between social reality and its political interpretation. They testify to a latent malaise whose consequences, even without Adolf Hitler, would have led to major social and political transformation. This need not have led to war and Auschwitz. But with high probability, it would have been fatal to the Weimar Republic in the form envisaged by the authors of its constitution.

National Socialism was not the cause of the malaise, nor was its ultimate totalitarian, imperialist form the inevitable consequence. Its programmatic demands were neither original nor peculiar to Hitler's Party. The Nazis came to power by miscalculation rather than by some exclusive popular demand focusing on the person of Hitler or his Party. The mandate with which Hitler took office was a conglomerate of disparities and contradictions long apparent to anyone interested in politics, both outside the party and in it. The common denominator of Nazi appeal was as remote as the smile of the Cheshire cat. In its negative form, it was a promise to make things different, in its positive form, a promise to make things better. But as far removed as it was from the unitary political will Hitler claimed to see in the uniform columns of the SA (Sturmabteilung—Storm Troopers, "brown shirts") or the ecstatic acclamation of a mass audience, there was in it nonetheless a homogencity great enough to cover the yawning cracks in the Party program with ballot papers. This was the homogencity of common disaffection.

The disaffection was structural, endemic in all Western industrial societies, but intensified in Germany by special historical factors: a non-competitive, highly concentrated, high-priced industrial economy, the disproportionate influence of a small class of large landowners, a high birthrate until World War I, too many rural smallholders, an inflated urban petite bourgeoisie. All of these had been built into Bismarck's Reich. Carried along on the winds of economic expansion, they formed a fair-weather constellation whose stability was virtually identical with the success of its political leadership in balancing the conflicting demands and requirements of industry and agriculture, labor and capital, West and East, centralism and particularism, Catholic and Protestant, rich and poor. Success created a clientele that included even the nominal enemies of the established order. Their own vested interest in this order was certainly an important factor in the SPD (Social Democrat) decision to vote war credits in 1914. But the compromises of the old order failed to solve, even precluded solving, the problems of an industrial society. The collapse of the monarchy in 1918 with its chaotic "return to normalcy" only reintroduced the problems of the prewar era after four uneasy years of civil truce. But they were now complicated by the by-products of defeat: a "lost generation" of demobilized soldiers; a floating population of eastern refugees, many of them aristocrats; the liquidation of millions of war loans floated with middle-class savings; and a large disproportion in the demographic relationship of women to men. Finally, there were the economic consequences of the war: reparations, loss of export markets, exhaustion of both plant and raw materials, and inflation. The latent social problems of the prewar era were further complicated by a crisis of legitimacy in the political order coinciding with economic disintegration. The results were paradoxical, on the one hand, consistent and uninterrupted extension of the social tendencies of the prewar era, on the other, an ideologized misinterpretation of these tendencies that effectively prevented the solution of the maladjustments they caused.

A statistical résumé leaves no doubt about the unambiguous course of social development (see Table 1).

TABLE 1. German Occupational Distribution in % of Population

Year	Agriculture	Industry and handicrafts	Services
1882	42	36	22
1895	36	39	25
1907	34	40	26
1925	30	42	28
1933	29	41	30

This was the classical pattern of industrialization, urban growth, industrial rationalization, and the development of distribution and service industries. While only 5 per cent of the German population had lived in cities of over 100,000 in 1871, the proportion had grown by 1925 to 27 per cent. Equally striking was the relative redistribution of ownership and economic status (see Table 2).

TABLE 2. German Occupational Status in % of Population

In %	1882	1895	1907	1925	1933
Independent	38	35	27	21	20
Their employed dependents	4	4	8	10	11
White collar including civil service	8	11	14	19	18
Workers	50	50	51	50	52

While the figures were neutral as economic indicators—pointing only to advancing industrialization and relative only to success in feeding, housing, and clothing an industrial population—they were full of implications as a reflection of social and political tendencies. The loss of economic independence, the employment of family members, the ballooning white collar population characteristic both of the big city and the bureaucratic state and economy all affected the self-respect of the people they touched—or at least were capable of doing so as soon as they seemed to coincide with a decline in the standard of living. If the processes themselves were characteristic of capitalism, it stood to reason that those affected by them would come to consider themselves anti-capitalistic, without, however, accepting the theoretical Marxian implications of their misery and disappearing in the traditional proletariat. Theodor Geiger estimated, on the basis of the 1925 census, that 25,000,000 Germans could be classed, socially, as proletarians. But 45,000,000, roughly three quarters of the population were living—during a period of increasing prosperity nearly five years before the depression—on proletarian incomes.

Particularly characteristic of this tendency were the retail traders, a bumper crop sown by the imperial order and in constant fear of being mowed down by the economics of the Republic. Between 1882 and 1907, the number of small retail traders had grown faster than both population and the national product as people sought to exploit urban growth and a rising living standard in tobacco shops, groceries, drugstores (Drogerien), and delicatessens (Feinkosgeschäfte). Even before the war, existing statistics pointed to a decline in professional quality. A survey of Brunswick grocers (Kolonialwarenhändler) in 1901 established that only 34 per cent had had any vocational training compared with 67 per cent in 1887. Even before the depression, the economic consequences of the peace had revealed the weaknesses of the small shopkeeper, exposed to the business cycle, unresponsive to shifting population, and inadequately trained for either successful competition or other employment. Added to his problem on the one hand were the price-sinking creations of advancing technology and concentrated capital, the chain and department stores, and on the other, the vast overaccumulation of non-competitive manpower in retail trade. Between 1907 and 1925, the number of retail outlets rose from 695,800 to 847,900, an increase of about 21 per cent. Between 1924 and 1929 it increased another 3 per cent. Geiger estimated that in 1925 nearly 45 per cent of those engaged in retail trade were already living on proletarian incomes.

Meanwhile the number of department store subsidiaries rose from 101 in 1925 to 176 in 1929. While their absolute share of retail turnover was still small enough, their relative share by 1928 was growing 22 per cent faster than the total volume of retail trade. Between 1925 and 1931 so-called "specialty" shops lost 5 per cent of their share of retail volume, a relatively small figure but one magnified by higher operating costs, lively imaginations, and then by the depression. A 1929 tax study showed that the department stores had, in fact, taken over only 4 per cent, the chain stores at most 1.1 per cent of retail trade. This included, however, up to 6 per cent of the turnover in clothing and 20 per cent in household goods and furniture. By 1928 retail pressure groups were pressing for increased taxes on department stores, a goal achieved by 1929 in Munich and Frankfurt, Main. In 1932, the Brüning government declared a limit on further department store expansion, followed before the year was out by a similar ban on chain stores. Whether his misery was caused by his own inefficiency, his aversion to co-operatives, to the methods, economics, or good advertising of larger units within his own line, or by the department stores was a matter of indifference to the retail merchant whose effective desire was a self-contradiction: free enterprise minus its attendant risks.

But while the economic implications of retail trade seemed to point in the direction of the Marxist prognosis, toward concentration, intensified competition, and the strangulation of the small, independent proprietor, another development pointed in the opposite direction. This was the rapid growth of the white-collar population, "sociologically perhaps the most significant development of the last decades," as Ferdinand Fried called it in 1931. It was indeed characteristic of the period that the white-collar workers formed one of the best-observed of all social groups, their origins, attitudes, and habits becoming a subject of considerable public interest. Siegfried Kracauer's Marxist phenomenology of the white-collar worker ran for weeks in a daily newspaper in 1929 while the white-collar "little-man" became in 1932 the hero of a fictional best seller, Hans Fallada's *Little Man, What Now?*

Coming as they did both from the ranks of the traditional bourgeoisie and from the proletariat, it was nonetheless clear that the white-collar workers were neither workers nor middle class in the traditional sense. Contemporary social science begged the problem of categorization rather than solved it by calling the entire group, from shop clerks to graduate engineers, "the new middle class." But this was hardly a guide to their behavior, which was, from the Marxist point of view from which they were most often observed, a collection of anomalies.

The white-collar worker was usually employed in a big city and by a big employer. He—or still more likely, she—was often of working-class origins, even before the war. Hans Speier quoted a number of surveys (see Table 3).

TABLE 3. Survey of White-Collar Worker Origins

Year	Job classification	Working class origins
1906	Berlin saleswomen	33.6%
1909–11	Young Munich saleswomen	66.9
1932	Cologne saleswomen	51.5
1929	Apprentices of Gewerkschaft der Angestellten (clerical union):	
	Male	33.6
	Female	42.9

White-collar workers showed a progressive tendency to organize, and in a relatively militant organization from which employers were excluded. But both the form and the objectives differed from the traditional union pattern, corresponding in part to the different social origins of the membership, in part to the nature of their employment. While Geiger estimated that less than 4 per cent of the working-class population was skilled (qualifiziert), he estimated that 70 per cent of the white-collar population had some professional qualifications. This alone might have led them away from the traditional union demands. While 80 per cent of the workers were organized in the so-called "free" socialist unions in 1931, only 25 per cent of the white-collar workers were organized in the socialist Gewerkschaft der Angestellten (clerical union), while 22.6 per cent were in the national-liberal Hirsch-Duncker unions and 34.1 per cent in the so-called "Christian-National" organizations like the Deutschnationaler-Handlungsgehilfenverband (German National Sales Clerks Association) (DHGV), perhaps the only economic-interest organization in Weimar Germany that combined a racist-nationalist (völkisch) program with mass membership. It is also of interest that 39 per cent of the DHGV membership came from working-class origins.

While the white-collar union was a tough negotiator and the pressure of economic circumstances could bring about a professional solidarity great enough to overcome the ideological divisions separating the white-collar groups, white-collar consciousness made itself felt in a preoccupation with salaries instead of wages, long-term contracts, and pensions; reflections of a concern with security—including the security of social status—that distinguished it from the blue-collar unions. Weimar legislation continued to distinguish white collar (Angestellten) from blue collar (Arbeiter), granting the former special job security, separate status in wage contracts, and a separate insurance fund.

Both Schumpeter and Lederer-Marschak claimed to see the line between blue collar and white collar fading, Schumpeter because the workers were coming to live like petits bourgeois, Lederer and Marschak because the white-collar workers were coming to behave like other workers. The depression proved the contrary. Unemployment hit blue collar and white collar alike, but psychologically it hit the white-collar worker harder. Speier quotes an unemployed white-collar worker: "... one is immediately ostracized, one is déclassé, without means of support, unemployed—that's equal to being a Communist." Déclassé is clearly the important word, reflecting a sensitivity of self-esteem different from that of the traditional working class. The increased employment of women—between 1913 and 1921 the proportion of women in the white-collar organizations had grown from 7.7 to 23.8 per cent—tended to increase the tension by making higher paid male jobs more vulnerable and compounding class war with sex war.

A key group in the white-collar population was an academically trained class, multiplied by postwar circumstances beyond its prewar numbers and increasingly absorbed in salaried employment in an economy that placed growing demands on technically trained manpower. The economic crises of the first Weimar years fell with particular weight on them, a group already sensitive to its exclusion, in part real, in part apparent, from traditional careers in the Army and civil service. While the social structure of Germany's political leadership changed significantly, the structure of the university population changed little except to the extent to which it grew and suffered. The 1922 *Who's Who* revealed that 20.3 per cent of the political entries came from the working class and 30.8 per cent from lower-income groups while only 40.8 per cent came from the old upper classes (Oberschicht). But the universities were peopled by the sons of the groups most conscious of the loss this revolution had caused them. The relative frequency of sons from the families of professional men went up in proportion to the restrictions imposed on business and the military. But while the sons of lawyers cautiously chose to make their ways in other areas, considerable numbers in medicine, pharmacy, and the natural sciences, the law faculties were filled with the sons of the petite bourgeoisie seeking the traditional prewar way to the top. In 1929, 23.4 percent of all students were from the families of university graduates, 11.5 per cent from the homes of the rich—big landowners, company directors, etc. But 64.2 per cent came from the middle class intent on making their way in a world whose political direction was increasingly dominated, as they would tend to see it, either by the discredited representatives of the old order or by their social and cultural inferiors.

"The age of the self-made man is past," Robert Michels claimed. The only career open to the talented working-class boy was political. At the same time there was every evidence of dissatisfaction in a university graduate population of 840,000 while the student population tended to grow by 10 per cent a year. Since the routes to the top narrowed, and the traffic increased, the result appeared to be fewer and fewer rewards for higher and higher qualifications. Fried, who clearly felt himself a victim of the process, was eloquent in his description of its consequences: four to six years of university study, costing from five to nine thousand marks, rewarded with starting salaries ranging from two to four hundred marks monthly and advancing to a level commensurate with family obligations and social status only when its recipient reached the age of forty or fifty. The university graduate, Fried declared, felt as he had once felt during his first weeks of military service: spiritually and physically exploited. But while he might once have become a reserve officer for his pains, his civilian occupation under present circumstances offered him the chance of one day becoming—with the best of luck—a prokurist, a kind of economic sergeant. "The way to the top is blocked off," he concluded, including among the obstacles the oligarchy of age. Reichstag deputies were, on the average, fifty-six years old, the two hundred leading economic figures, sixty-one years old—"rigid, dead, outdated and reactionary like the SPD."

One other major social group, the farmers, shared the general disaffection. Geiger estimated that nearly 60 per cent of them were living on proletarian incomes. The intensity and quality of their disaffection varied according to region and market conditions but was ultimately reducible to the classic problem of agriculture in an industrial society: the farmer's inability to control prices and production in an otherwise manipulable economy. The result was a curious dilemma. Massive economic disintegration might bring him short-term advantages, as it did during the 1923 inflation which liquidated his debts and brought him the short-term benefits of a barter economy and a sellers' market. But in the long run, the farmer suffered as the general economy suffered. On the other hand, prosperity, even as it brought him higher prices, tended to increase the lag between farm and industrial income on one side and farm and industrial prices on the other. His efforts to overcome this gap resulted in overproduction with a consequent decline in prices. . . .

None of these problems was new or unique to Germany. In one form or another they had been, since the middle of the nineteenth century, not only the raw material of German politics but in varying degrees of the politics of all industrial and industrializing countries. In America similar phenomena had fueled political controversy since at least the election of Jackson in 1828 and formed the bases of the mass Populist and Progressive movements before World War I and later the basis of the New Deal.

What complicated solution in Germany was not a failure to recognize the structural inadequacies of industrial society, but rather a failure to find an alternative social model adequate to correct them. Advancing literacy, urbanization, industrialization, and the development of overseas agriculture all pointed to the liberal society envisaged by the Weimar Convention. But the main currents of social thought since at least the constitution of the Reich pointed away from it. They aimed instead at what René König calls "the two revolutions that didn't occur." One of these was Marxist. The other was what Fritz Stern has called "the politics of cultural despair," a kind of Peter Pan ideology for a society that didn't want to grow up. As aware as the Marxists of the evils of industrialization, the cultural pessimists saw their correction not so much in a redistribution of ownership as in the elimination of industrial society itself. They waged war against the city, turned rural emigration into the pejorative "Landflucht" as though it were a form of desertion, created a distinction between Gemeinschaft, the Arcadian community of the rural village, and Gesellschaft, the soulless rat race of urban society, and turned the sociological discussion of the period into an exhaustive analysis of "class" and "estate." The homestead act of 1919 and the economic parliament foreseen by the Weimar Constitution were testimony to their influence even during the brief honeymoon of popular support for the liberal Republic. In the form of land reform and conventions of estates (Ständekammern) and supplemented with demands for industrial profit sharing, nationalization of trusts, and redistribution of department store properties to small business, both measures found their echo only a few months later in the "inalterable" Nazi program of 24 February 1920.

This was less evidence of Nazi originality than of the Zeitgeist. The infant Party was obliged to climb on the bandwagon to remain in the race. What subsequently turned the NSDAP into a mass organization with a voter potential of fourteen million, and finally into Germany's governing Party, was at no point its programmatic command of the issues or pseudo-issues, but its manipulation of them. It was the mobilization of disaffection.

A form of this general disaffection had created National Socialism even before Hitler discovered it. In its original form, National Socialism was a phenomenon of the South German border areas, an organization of "little men," frequently handicraftsmen, frequently of small-town origin, all of them hungry for the respect of their German-National social betters. An outline of its general premises can be found in the unassuming autobiographical essay of Anton Drexler, the chairman of the little German Workers Party Hitler discovered in Munich in 1919. Drexler described with horror his youthful experiences in Berlin, his ostracism for unstated reasons by Socialist unionists, and the humiliation of having to play the zither in a restaurant. With the querulousness of the born crank, he was quick to find a Jewish-capitalist-Masonic conspiracy at the root of all problems, to appreciate its diabolical exploitation of existing class differences to plunge Germany unprepared into World War I and then to secure its defeat. While addressing himself to the working class, he was careful to avoid offense, to declare the worker a Bürger, and the officer and civil servant non-bourgeois. He declared himself in favor of capitalism but "healthy" capitalism, and drew a line between the Bürger, the farmer, the worker, and the soldier, on one side, and their common enemy, the capitalist Jew, on the other.

In industrially underdeveloped Munich at the end of the war and after the left-wing putsch that followed it, this was an ideology with a certain appeal. The following it attracted was not limited as Hitler later tried to suggest. Hitler, who joined with membership card No. 555, found both a rudimentary party program and a potentially expansive membership. The ideology was the work of a kind of Central European William Jennings Bryan, the engineer Gottfried Feder, whose specialty was inflationary fiscal policy and who had previously tried without success to sell his schemes to Kurt Eisner, the Socialist leader of the 1918 Bavarian revolution. The membership was mixed, in part a combination of desperate small shopkeepers, professional men, and workers like the machinist Drexler and his friends from the railroad, in part of demobilized soldiers like Hitler himself, at loose ends and unable to find their way back into civilian life. There being potentially large reserves in both the "civilian" and the "military" groups, this was a combination with a political future, provided that it found leadership capable of holding it together, and that economic and political stabilization did not undermine its attractiveness. . . .

While the Nazi vote for the Reichstag fell in 1928 to 810,000, or ninth in order of representation, the creation and combination of ideological clienteles—Feder's petite bourgeoisie, Rosenberg's cultural pessimists, Goebbels' and the Strassers' young activists—and, above all, the charisma of Hitler, sustained both a base and an image. Radical, youthful, anti-Communist, sympathetic to small business, not necessarily hostile to big business, and ferociously nationalistic, the Party, like its program, was potentially acceptable in one way or another to nearly every large social group. Even while the vote fell, membership rose steadily—from 27,000 in 1925 to 178,000 in 1929. National Socialism had its hard core, a sociological base more diversified than that of any other party except the Catholic Center (Zentrum), variously maintained by fear of the department store, fear of communism, fear of the Poles, fear of further decline in the price of farm commodities, and "the politics of cultural despair." The numbers were small but tenacious; the cadres were there.

On the eve of its first great election victory on 14 September 1930, the Party consisted of:

workers	26.3%
white collar	24.0
independent	18.9
civil servants	7.7
farmers	13.2
miscellaneous	9.9

Still more revealing of its sources of support was its age distribution:

18–20	0.4%
21–30	36.4
31–40	31.4
41–50	17.6
51–60	9.7
61–	4.5

In the Party groups in Berlin, Halle-Merseburg, Mecklenburg-Lübeck, the Palatinate, and Württemberg-Hohenzollern, the 21 to 30 year-olds were more than 40 per cent of the total membership. In comparison to the average for the Reich, the under-developed areas of South Germany, Lower Bavaria, Franconia, the Palatinate, and Schleswig-Holstein with its chronic agricultural crisis were overrepresented.

The Nazi deputies elected to the Reichstag in September 1930—who, under Weimar's proportional electoral system, were men who had distinguished them-selves in the Party apparatus rather than men with direct public appeal—included, by their own identification, 16 in crafts, trade, or industry; 25 employees, both blue- and white-collar workers; 13 teachers; 12 career civil servants; 9 editors and 6 Party employees, together 15 full-time Party functionaries; 8 military officers; a Protestant clergyman; and a druggist, Gregor Strasser; as well as 12 engaged in agriculture. Of the 107, 12 were under 30 (compared with 8 of the 77 KPD deputies), 59 between 30 and 40 (compared with 45 of the 77 KPD deputies, 17 of the 143 SPD deputies). Roughly 60 per cent of the Nazi (and KPD) deputies were under 40, compared with scarcely more than 10 per cent from the SPD.

Hitler's course from here to the Machtergreifung (seizure of power) was, even more than before, tactically rather than ideologically defined. As Weimar's social and political supports collapsed under the impact of the depression, his object, as before, was effectively negative: to do nothing that might antagonize potential sup-port. This went so far, as Theodor Heuss noted, as to exclude Jews as the favored target. Hitler had nothing against "decent" Jews, he is supposed to have told a foreign visitor after the September election, and Heuss had the impression that Goebbels' characterization of bourgeois opponents as a "stinking dung heap" caused him genu-ine embarrassment. Even before the election, Otto Strasser—a "utopian socialist," as he considered himself—left the Party, antagonized by a series of what he felt to be officially sanctioned harassments and outraged, he reported, by Hitler's evident opportunism. There was no such thing as social or economic revolution, Hitler is supposed to have told him, redistribution of ownership was a Marxist chimera, the economy in its existing form was inviolable, and socialism meant nothing more than State intervention to assure the prevention of conflict. He even rejected autarky. "Do you think we can isolate ourselves from the world economy?" he asked. Nazis were forbidden to join a strike in Saxony in April 1930, another of Strasser's sore points. In October 1930 when the dimensions of a metalworkers' strike in Berlin made this impossible, the Party dispatched its economic advisor, the retired major Otto Wagener, to persuade Saxon industrialists that the alternative was a mass migration to the SPD. Officially Hitler announced in the *Völkische Beobachter* that participation in the strike was intended to teach German industry a lesson in the consequences of observing the conditions of the Versailles Treaty.

At the same time, the Party permitted itself occasional displays of its old radical-ism. On 14 October 1930, the newly elected Reichstag deputation presented a bill demanding confiscation of all bank and brokerage fortunes, of the property of all East European Jews who had arrived in Germany since 1914 and of all profits accru-ing from the war or speculation, as well as nationalization of the larger banks and a maximum interest rate of 4 per cent. But they withdrew it in the face of the SPD and KPD who threatened to support it, knowing this would frighten Hitler's financial supporters, and equally in the face of Germany's economists who bought newspaper space to testify to the bill's impracticability. In early 1931 a bill in the budget committee of the Reichstag forbidding the acquisition of any further public debts and the financing of all public works with interest-free Reich credit bills testified to the survival of Feder's influence and the old populist spirit. So, in May 1932, did Strasser's famous proclamation of the *antikapitalistische Schnsucht* (anticapitalist yearning), with its demands that Germany go off the gold standard, increase its farm productivity, break up its urban concentrations, create a rural labor service, control farm prices and wages, finance cheap credits, and lower interest rates.

But Hitler's course led away from specific demands rather than toward them, even at the risk of offending potential radical support like the SA, which was already susceptible to mutiny, or like the young Reichswehr lieutenant Richard Scheringer whose indignation about the Party's apparently anti-revolutionary course led him in 1931 to make a public switch to the KPD. The Party was becoming respectable, and Hitler, concerned very much with votes and financial support and very little with ideological consistency, did his best to ease and hasten the process. Fritz Thyssen reported later that Hitler had given him the impression that he intended to clear the way for a restoration of the monarchy, while the young and foolish Prince of Schaumburg-Lippe told of Hitler's assurance that his movement had room for monarchists and republicans alike. Thyssen agreed to underwrite the Party. Schaumburg-Lippe volunteered to campaign actively in its support and noted by 1931–32 that his relatives—one of the Kaiser's sons among them—already had not only accepted "high and highest" positions in the party and SA but had been sent ahead as Landtag and Reichstag deputies. Krebs, at the same time, noted that the later Hamburg Gauleiter Karl Kaufmann, then close to the Strasserite wing of the Hamburg Party, had been censured from Munich for his critique of Hitler's "Harzburg Front" with Alfred Hugenberg and the Stahlhelm, and that he himself was being edged out of his position as press secretary of the Party by a man with the "best connections" to the Hamburg merchant bourgeoisie.

Still presented in their "inviolability," the twenty-five points of the Party program were meanwhile subjected to a creeping violation intended to reduce any remaining resistance in yet untapped electoral reservoirs. As early as 1928 Hitler had replied to a challenge from the farmers' organizations by declaring that the land reform envisaged in the Party program would not lead to expropriations. The phrase "uncompensated expropriation," he stated, referred only to Jewish speculators. The Party stood firmly in support of private property. In its practical activity, the Party went still further. When the SPD in Brunswick presented a bill granting the state automatic priority of purchase right in sales of land, a bill whose language was copied directly from Rosenberg's official exposition of the land-reform paragraph in the Party program, eight of the nine Nazi deputies voted against it. As early as 1928, this combination of tactical accommodation with falling prices resulted in a steep climb in rural support, particularly in hitherto untapped North and East German Protestant areas.

Appealing to the middle class, Feder confined the problem of profitsharing to the very largest industrial concentrations like the I. G. Farben, then redefined it as simple price-reduction, which would bring its benefits to everyone, rather than confining it to employees of the firm concerned. He also distinguished between "moral" industrialists and "anonymous, depersonalized" corporations. Rosenberg left the problem to the future. Still more important than ideological concessions was political organization in the form of the Kampfbund für den gewerblichen Mittelstand (Small Business Action League), another fellow-traveler group, under the leadership of Theodor Ardian von Renteln, earlier the Party's first youth leader. The organizing of fellow travelers was meanwhile extended to every other possible interest group—to lawyers, doctors, teachers, schoolboys, and to women whose organizers were instructed to avoid titles, uniforms, and class appeals, and to concentrate instead on Christianity, motherhood, and the family as the basis of the future Reich. Hung above each subappeal—fixed prices for the farmers, jobs for the unemployed, liberation from competition with big competitors for small business, and careers open to talent for the young—was the general appeal of "Rescue Germany," an idealized form of "sauve qui peut," as Geiger said, directed at a population that had lost the selfconfidence of 1848 and 1870 and was now prepared to throw itself into the arms of its own desperation. Underpinning it was a style composed equally of radical activism, military hierarchy, and the grandiose hocus-pocus of a fraternal lodge, embellished with stars, stripes, oak leaves, medals, and badges. Hitler's Party had become a revolutionary mass organization whose members addressed one another with the formal, plural "Sie" rather than the familiar "Du." . . .

Seen against its social background, National Socialism is far too complicated a phenomenon to be derived from any single source or reduce to any single common denominator, whether it be the depression or the course of German history. Its very dynamism precluded easy generalizations. If, before 1930, the NSDAP tended to be a Party of völkisch true believers, like the Göttingen Nazis who saw their mission in the compilation of a directory of Jews in German academic life, it tended after 1930 to be an organization of the economically desperate with a considerable admixture of opportunism. "When I joined the NSDAP," Fritzsche testified at Nuremberg, "I did not have the impression of joining a Party in the conventional sense since this was a Party without a theory. . . . All the Party theoreticians were under fire. . . . There were already whole groups of former DNVP members in the NSDAP or of former Communists. . . ."

"The formula, 'National Socialism is exclusively that which So-and-so says or does,' whereby the particular proponent was referring to himself, replaced the Party program . . . ," Hans Frank declared in his memoirs. "Any number of names filled the formula at the start: Hitler, Goering, Strasser, Röhm, Goebbels, Hess, Rosenberg, and more. There were as many National Socialisms as there were leaders."

The most general theory—that National Socialism was a revolution of the lower middle class—is defensible but inadequate. National Socialism had a striking appeal for the Auslandsdeutsche, Germans who had spent the impressionable years of their lives in a German community abroad. Whether at the microcosmic level of the Göttingen Party or in important positions in Munich, like Rosenberg or Darré, there was an impressive number of them. National Socialism was no less a revolt of the young against the old. While a theory of National Socialism as a lower middle-class phenomenon applies very well to voter behavior, it fails to account for important sectors of Party leadership with their violent animosity toward the social forms for which their voters yearned. Himmler's contempt for the bourgeois self-indulgence of railway dining cars was no more a lower middle-class attitude than the longing for action, power, nights of the long knives, or a radical reorganization of society, shared by the Party's leaders. National Socialism drew unmistakably on the historical reserves of liberal support, but its leaders were unequivocally sworn to the destruction of liberal values and liberal society.

This hard core of revolutionary destructiveness existed before the depression in quantities too great to be dismissed as simple personal idiosyncrasy. The longing for security that it exploited existed before the depression as well, but sought its objectives elsewhere in unrevolutionary places. What brought them together, leaders and followers, was a common hostility to the status quo at a moment of unique desperation, a desperation only two parties, the KPD and the NSDAP were fully prepared to exploit. In promising everything to everybody, the Nazis promised nothing to anybody. The tactical pursuit of power obviated any immediate urgency in the discussion of what was to be done once it was attained. As it was to Frank and Fritzsche this was clear to the farmer who told Heberle ". . . we believe that in the Third Reich, we, the farmers, will be so strong a power that we can shape it as we desire." From a contemporary standpoint, National Socialism was wide open, its disparity not a handicap but a positive advantage. What united it ultimately was not a mandate for war and Auschwitz, but a universal desire for change.

The Doctrine of Fascism

Benito Mussolini

*Benito Mussolini—former schoolteacher, journalist, and WWI veteran—
was the main figure in the Italian political movement known as "Fascism,"
a term he coined. Mussolini and the Fascists seized power during the 1920s,
which they held until Italy was liberated by Allied forces during World War
Two.*

When, in the now distant March of 1919, I summoned a meeting at Milan . . . of the
surviving members of the interventionist Party who had themselves been in action,
and who had followed me since the creation of the Fascist Revolutionary Party (of
1915), I had no specific doctrinal attitude in mind. I had a living experience of one
doctrine only—that of Socialism, from 1903–4 to the winter of 1914—that is to say,
about a decade; and from Socialism itself, even though I have taken part in the movement first as a member of the rank and file and later as a leader, yet I had no experience of its doctrine of action. A unanimous, universally accepted theory of Socialism
did not exist after 1905. . . . In the great stream of Fascism are to be found ideas
which began with Sorel, Peguy, with Lagardelle in the "Mouvement Socialiste," and
with the Italian trade union movement which throughout the period of 1904–14 was
sounding a new note in Italian Socialist circles. . . .

After the war, in 1919, Socialism was already dead as a doctrine; it existed only
as hatred. The *Popolo d'Italia* was then given the subtitle of "The newspaper of ex-
servicemen and producers," and the word "producers" was already the expression of
a mental attitude. Fascism was not the nursling of a doctrine worked out beforehand
with detailed elaboration; it was born of the need for action and it was itself from the
beginning practical rather than theoretical; it was not merely another political party
but, even in the first two years, in opposition to all political parties as such. . . . If one
were to re-read . . . the report of the meeting in which the *Fasci Italiani di combat-
timento* were constituted, one would there find no ordered expression of doctrine,
but a series of aphorisms, anticipations, and aspirations which, when refined by time
from the original ore, were destined after some years to develop into an ordered
series of doctrinal concepts, forming the Fascists' political doctrine—different from
all others either of the past or the present day.

"If the bourgeoisie," I said then, "think that they will find lightning-rods in us, they are the more deceived; we must start work at once. . . . We want to accustom the working class to real and effectual leadership, and also to convince them that it is no easy thing to direct an industry or a commercial enterprise successfully. . . . We shall combat every retrograde idea, technical or spiritual. . . . When the succession to the seat of government is open, we must not be unwilling to fight for it. We must make haste; when the present regime breaks down, we must be ready at once to take its place. It is we who have the right to the succession, because it was we who forced the country into the War, and led her to victory. The present method of political representation cannot suffice, we must have a representation direct from the individuals concerned. It may be objected against this program that it is a return to the conception of the corporation, but that is no matter. . . . Therefore, I desire that this assembly shall accept the claims of national trades-unionism from the economic point of view. . . ."

Now is it not a singular thing that even on this first day in the Piazza San Sepolcro that word "corporation" arose, which later, in the course of the Revolution, came to express one of the creations of social legislation at the very foundation of the regime?

The years which preceded the March to Rome were years of great difficulty, during which the necessity for action did not permit of research or any complete elaboration of doctrine. The battle had to be fought in the towns and villages. There was much discussion, but—what was more important and more sacred—men died. They knew how to die. Doctrine, beautifully defined and carefully elucidated, with headlines and paragraphs, might be lacking; but there was to take its place something more decisive—Faith. . . . But, since there was inevitably some lack of system, the adversaries of Fascism have disingenuously denied that it had any capacity to produce a doctrine of its own, though that doctrine was growing and taking shape under their very eyes, even though tumultuously; first, as happens to all ideas in their beginnings, in the aspect of a violent and dogmatic negation, and then in the aspect of positive construction which has found its realization in the laws and institutions of the regime as enacted successively in the years 1926, 1927, and 1928. . . .

Above all, Fascism, the more it considers and observes the future and the development of humanity quite apart from political considerations of the moment, believes neither in the possibility nor the utility of perpetual peace. It thus repudiates the doctrine of Pacifism—born of a renunciation of the struggle and an act of cowardice in the face of sacrifice. War alone brings up to its highest tension all human energy and puts the stamp of nobility upon the peoples who have the courage to meet it. All other trials are substitutes, which never really put men into the position where they have to make the great decision—the alternative of life or death. Thus a doctrine which is founded upon this harmful postulate of peace is hostile to Fascism. And thus hostile to the spirit of Fascism . . . are all the international leagues and societies, which, as history will show, can be scattered to the winds when once strong national feeling is aroused by any motive—sentimental, ideal, or practical. This anti-pacifist spirit is carried by Fascism even into the life of the individual; the proud motto of the Squadrista, "*Me ne frego*" (I do not hear), written on the bandage of the wound, is an act of philosophy not only stoic, the summary of a doctrine not only political—it is the education to combat, the acceptance of the risks which combat implies, and a new way of life for Italy. Thus the Fascist accepts life and loves it, knowing nothing of and despising suicide; he rather conceives of life as duty and struggle and conquest, life which should be high and full, lived for oneself, but above all for others—those who are at hand and those who are far distant, contemporaries, and those who will come after. . . ."

Such a conception of life makes Fascism the complete opposite of that doctrine, the base of the so-called scientific and Marxian Socialism, the materialist conception of history; according to which the history of human civilization can be explained simply through the conflict of interests among the various social groups and by the change and development in the means and instruments of production. That the changes in the economic field . . . have their importance no one can deny; but that these factors are sufficient to explain the history of humanity excluding all others is an absurd delusion. Fascism, now and always, believes in holiness and heroism; that is to say, in actions influenced by no economic motive, direct or indirect. And if the economic conception of history be denied . . . it follows that the existence of an unchangeable and unchanging class war is also denied. And above all Fascism denies that class war can be the preponderant force in the transformation of society. These two fundamental concepts of Socialism being thus refuted, nothing is left of it but the sentimental aspiration—as old as humanity itself—towards a social convention in which the sorrows and sufferings of the humblest shall be alleviated. But here again Fascism repudiates the conception of economic happiness. . . . Fascism denies the materialist conception of happiness as a possibility, and abandons it to its inventors, the economists of the first half of the nineteenth century: that is to say, Fascism denies the validity of the equation, well-being=happiness, which would reduce men to the level of animals, caring for one thing only—to be fat and well-fed—and would thus degrade humanity to a purely physical existence.

After Socialism, Fascism combats the whole complex system of democratic ideology; and repudiates it, whether in its theoretical premises or in its practical application. Fascism denies that the majority, by the simple fact that it is a majority, can direct human society; it denies that numbers alone can govern by means of a periodical consultation, and it affirms the immutable, beneficial, and fruitful inequality of mankind, which can never be permanently leveled through the mere operation of a mechanical process such as universal suffrage. The democratic regime may be defined as from time to time giving the people the illusion of sovereignty, while the real effective sovereignty lies in the hands of other concealed and irresponsible forces. Democracy is a regime nominally without a king, but it is ruled by many kings—more absolute, tyrannical, and ruinous than one sole king, even though a tyrant. This explains why Fascism, having first in 1922 (for reasons of expediency) assumed an attitude tending towards republicanism, renounced this point of view before the March to Rome; being convinced that the question of political form is not today of prime importance. . . .

A party which entirely governs a nation is a fact entirely new to history, there are no possible references or parallels. Fascism uses in its construction whatever elements in the Liberal, Social, or Democratic doctrines still have a living value; it maintains what may be called the certainties which we owe to history, but it rejects all the rest—that is to say, the conception that there can be any doctrine of unquestioned efficacy for all times and all peoples. . . . Political doctrines pass, but humanity remains; and it may rather be expected that this will be a century of Fascism. For if the nineteenth century was the century of individualism (Liberalism always signifying individualism) it may be expected that this will be the century of collectivism, and hence the century of the State. . . .

Every doctrine tends to direct human activity towards a determined objective; but the action of men also reacts upon the doctrine, transforms it, adapts it to new needs, or supersedes it with something else. A doctrine then must be no mere exercise in words, but a living act; and thus the value of Fascism lies in the fact that it is veined with pragmatism, but at the same time has a will to exist and a will to power, a firm front in face of the reality of "violence."

The foundation of Fascism is the conception of the State. Fascism conceives of the State as an absolute, in comparison with which all individuals or groups are relative, only to be conceived of in their relation to the State. . . .

The Fascist State has drawn into itself even the economic activities of the nation, and through the corporative social and educational institutions created by it, its influence reaches every aspect of the national life and includes, framed in their respective organizations, all the political, economic and spiritual forces of the nation. A State which reposes upon the support of millions of individuals who recognize its authority, are continually conscious of its power and are ready at once to serve it, is not the old tyrannical State of the medieval lord nor has it anything in common with the absolute governments either before or after 1789. The individual in the Fascist State is not annulled but rather multiplied, just in the same way that a soldier in a regiment is not diminished but rather increased by the number of his comrades. The Fascist State organizes the nation, but leaves a sufficient margin of liberty to the individual; that latter is deprived of all useless and possibly harmful freedom, but retains what is essential. . . .

The Fascist State is an embodied will to power and government; the Roman tradition is here an ideal of force in action. According to Fascism, government is not so much a thing to be expressed in territorial or military terms as in terms of morality and the spirit. It must be thought of as an empire—that is to say, a nation which directly or indirectly rules other nations, without the need for conquering a single square yard of territory. For Fascism, the growth of empire, that is to say the expansion of the nation, is an essential manifestation of vitality, and its opposite a sign of decadence. Peoples which are rising, or rising again after a period of decadence, are always imperialist; any renunciation is a sign of decay and of death.

Fascism is the doctrine best adapted to represent the tendencies and the aspirations of a people, like the people of Italy, who are rising again after many centuries of abasement and foreign servitude. But empire demands discipline, the co-ordination of all forces and a deeply felt sense of duty and sacrifice; this fact explains many aspects of the practical working of the regime, the character of many forces in the State, and the necessarily severe measures which must be taken against those who would oppose this spontaneous and inevitable movement of Italy in the twentieth century, and would oppose it by recalling the outworn ideology of the nineteenth century . . . for never before has the nation stood more in need of authority, of direction, and of order. If every age has its own characteristic doctrine, there are a thousand signs which point to Fascism as the characteristic doctrine of our time. For if a doctrine must be a living thing, this is proved by the fact that Fascism has created a living faith; and that this faith is very powerful in the minds of men, is demonstrated by those who have suffered and died for it.

Think About What You Saw: The Holocaust and Social Science

John W. Mackey

Signs prominently posted at the United States Holocaust Memorial Museum in Washington, D.C. make a simple yet perhaps weighty request of the museum's visitors:

"THINK ABOUT WHAT YOU SAW."[1]

The curators of the museum undoubtedly want their visitors to think about what they saw for at least two reasons: first, to remember and pay respects to the victims of the Holocaust, and second, to gain better insight into what actually happened, hopefully helping to prevent such brutality from occurring again.

While the scale of the horror may sometimes seem overwhelming or even incomprehensible, as human beings, and as students of history and social science, it is our task to try to understand. Throughout our social science courses this year, we have endeavored to understand how modern societies work, to understand the relationships between individuals, groups, and their societies, and understand the history of Western modernization. We may gain more insight into the nature of the Holocaust by applying some of the concepts and some of the history we have learned in our courses this year. And like visitors to the Holocaust museum, we should not only accept that the Holocaust happened, but we should *think* about it.

This request is more difficult and complicated than it may seem. For the Holocaust raises extremely difficult, troubling, confusing, and controversial questions. Ever since the first studies of the Holocaust, the subject has presented problems for historians and sociologists who have tried to make sense of it. In Germany, a very public argument about the Holocaust known as the **historikerstreit** ("historians' quarrel") is evidence of the disputed nature of this most troubling historical event.

While there is no single, agreed upon interpretation of the Holocaust, there are certain points that are beyond reasonable doubt. First, the Holocaust *happened*. **Holocaust deniers,** as they are often called, claim either that the Holocaust never happened, or that it has been greatly exaggerated and distorted. Such claims do not have merit. In fact, vast amounts of documentary evidence, physical evidence, and eyewitness testimony confirms the horrors perpetrated by the Nazis. The **concentration camps** existed, and the Nazis attempted to exterminate Jews, by far the most numerous victims, as well as others they considered undesirable or inferior, including Slavs, Romani, homosexuals, communists, and the disabled.

A second unavoidable point is that the Holocaust was deeply connected to and motivated by **anti-Semitism,** or the irrational hatred of Jews. From their rise to power in 1933, **Adolf Hitler** and the Nazi leadership targeted Jews for oppression, stripping them of basic rights and opportunities, and denouncing them as foreign, corrupting, and even sub-human in their rhetoric. Nazi ideology posited the idea that the Jews were the antithesis of the so-called **Aryan race,** a mythical master race associated with northern Europe, and sometimes with the German people more specifically. The condition of Jews in Germany worsened throughout the 1930s, until finally, during World War II, the decision to pursue a path of **genocide**—an attempt to exterminate the Jews—was reached. This decision, known by the grotesque Nazi euphemism **"The Final Solution to the Jewish Question,"** led to the mass murder of six million people.

Beyond these two points—that the Holocaust indeed occurred on a massive scale, and that it occurred in a climate of systematic, vehement anti-Semitism—it is more difficult to find consensus about the causes and nature of this human catastrophe. Below are two of the challenging but important questions raised by the Holocaust. The first examines the Holocaust in the historical context of the modernization of the West, the over-arching theme of our social science course this semester, and asks how this event can be interpreted in that context. The second focuses on the motivations and actions of individuals, and asks how we might explain how ordinary Germans carried out extraordinary acts of brutality on such a massive scale. In each case, potential answers for these questions are proposed. Which of the answers and social-science approaches below is most helpful in aiding our understanding of the Holocaust?

QUESTION ONE

Was the Holocaust the logical result of the process of modernization?

Western culture, especially since the Enlightenment of the eighteenth century, has often been deeply imbued with a sense of progress—a belief that historical change was trending in a positive direction, toward ever more sophistication, technology, economic development, and political freedom. But the horrors of the Holocaust might give pause to even the most ardent proponents of modernization and progress. Thus, our first question asks us to consider how the Holocaust fits into our understanding of modernization. Below are two possible answers to this question.

First potential answer: *Yes—the Holocaust was a logical, direct outcome of the processes of modernization.*

According to this argument, forces, processes, and institutions central to the modernization of Europe led directly to the Holocaust.

One element of this argument focuses on **science** and **technology.** The seventeenth-century scientific revolution and the eighteenth-century Enlightenment transformed the intellectual life of the west, replacing revelation, tradition, and common sense with inductive and deductive reasoning as sources of truth and knowledge, or **ways of knowing.** Scientific inquiry, along with new discoveries and inventions, in turn led to an explosion of technological change in the west, especially since the early nineteenth century.

Both of these trends—technological change and an increasingly scientific culture—can be linked to the events of the Holocaust. Scientific enthusiasm for studying and categorizing virtually all phenomena led to the creation of **"scientific" racism** in the nineteenth century. And the resultant categorization, indeed the *ranking* of human beings according to supposedly inherent and immutable racial distinctions, deeply influenced the Nazi worldview. The racial anti-Semitism and master-race ideology that fueled the Final Solution can thus be viewed as an outgrowth of trends in western science. That such racism has been thoroughly discredited by subsequent science does not alter the fact that, in its day, "scientific" racism was considered mainstream, rigorously researched, and valid.

The case for the contribution of applied science and technology to the slaughter is perhaps even more direct. Without the development and deployment of modern, and in some cases cutting-edge technology, the Nazis would never have been able to carry out genocide so rapidly on such a massive scale. Everything from trains (themselves a product of the historically recent Industrial Revolution), to communications technology, to newly developed chemicals made the Holocaust possible. Put simply, the gas chambers and the means of operating them and supplying them relied on modern industry and technology. Even **medical science,** ostensibly one of the most benevolent and life-giving of all human endeavors, was enlisted to help perpetrate the horrors of the concentration camps.

Another facet of the argument that the Holocaust was the outcome of modernization focuses on the development of the **modern nation state.** Nazism can be seen at its core as an extreme form of the modern ideology of **nationalism.** Indeed, the unification of the German state itself was the product of the nationalist fervor that swept through Europe in the nineteenth century. Nazism employed nationalist language and symbolism to instill a sense of obedience, duty, and sacrifice into the German people, mobilizing them on a massive scale.

As they promoted their extreme form of nationalism, the Nazi leadership proved to be experts in crafting and disseminating nationalist messages, through skillful use of another modern tool—**mass media.** Thus, led by Propaganda Minister Joseph Goebbels, the Nazis used film and other visual arts, mass rallies, parades, literature, periodicals, and other means to popularize nationalist **propaganda.** Public education and rising literacy rates, along with the invention of radio, television, and film gave twentieth-century governments new means and new opportunities to reach their citizens. Perhaps no other political party or movement took advantage of such opportunities more effectively than the Nazis. In countless ways, including the films of Leni Riefenstahl, art celebrating the "Aryan" form, and massive rallies and spectacles, the Nazis expertly manipulated words and images to create a startlingly effective and modern nationalist propaganda machine.

Such nationalist propaganda, when combined with anti-Semitism and other racialist messages, can be said to have laid the groundwork for the Holocaust. By defining Jews, Romani, homosexuals, or others considered undesirable by the Nazis as sub-human enemies of the Aryan race, Nazi propaganda turned mass murder into patriotic duty. For the sake of the nation, according to Nazi rhetoric, its enemies had to be eliminated.

And finally, another element of the modern nation state that helped to facilitate the Holocaust is **bureaucracy.** As the German sociologist Max Weber argued, the rationalization of power and authority into modern, bureaucratic structures enabled corporations and governments to carry out large-scale endeavors with efficiency and regularity.[2] And the Holocaust required massive logistical and organizational resources that arguably only a modern bureaucratic state could possibly provide. According to the sociologist Zygmunt Bauman, both the decisions that led to the drive for extermination of the Jews, and the procedures employed to accomplish this horrifying goal were ultimately a matter of "dull, bureaucratic routine."[3]

Thus, one point of view suggests that the horrors of the Holocaust were the product of modernity. Modern science and technology, modern nationalist and racist ideology, mass media, propaganda, and the rationalized, bureaucratic state all can be linked to the slaughter of millions of innocent victims by the Nazis. But another approach, which we will examine next, suggests something quite different; according to this view, the Holocaust can best be understood as an irrational rejection of the path of Western modernization.

Second potential answer: *No—the Holocaust was not the outcome of modernization, but an aberration, and/or an irrational rejection of modernity.*

According to this argument, the Holocaust and Nazism generally can best be understood not as a culmination of modernizing trends, but as a bizarre departure from the course of Western history, fueled by an irrational rejection of Enlightenment ideals.

This argument tends to focus on the anti-modern elements in Hitler's worldview, and their manifestations in Nazi culture and rhetoric. The Nazi vision of German greatness was a **romantic** one; the party employed rural, agrarian imagery to promote the idea of Germany as a racially pure nation of hard-working *volk* ("folk" or "people"), rooted to the soil. The Nazis considered modern urban life soulless and degenerate, and preferred to imagine Germany as a land where a mythical **Aryan race** of sturdy agrarian families served the nation with their labor. The Nazi state sought to replace the individualism of modern capitalist society, or *gesellschaft,* with a *volksgemeinschaft,* or "people's community."

Nazi ideology rejected **modern liberal politics** as well. Representative governments, parliamentary politics, reasoned debate, individual rights, and other Enlightenment-based institutions and values, according to the Nazis, were evidence of weakness and bourgeois decadence. Such weakness, they argued, was manifest in the failures of the parliamentary government of the **Weimar Republic,** which they held responsible for Germany's problems. The Nazis sought to build a state in which **action** would replace **reason,** and in which the imperatives of the nation would replace the rights and liberties of the individual. The Nazis urged the German people not to reason, reflect, and debate, but to take action by obeying their leader or *führer.* While reason and parliamentary politics led the nation to ruin, they argued, the *führer* would lead the nation to greatness. In fact, the modern political values of democrats, liberals, socialists, and communists were *all* rejected by the Nazis, rooted as they were in Enlightenment-inspired concepts.

Nazi ideology not only rejected modern economic systems, social organization, and politics, but modern, bourgeois culture as well. Germany had become a thriving center of modern art under the Weimar Republic, but the Nazis vehemently denounced virtually all forms of innovative, modern cultural expression. The works of many writers, musicians, and painters now considered modern masters—Kafka, Schoenberg, and Picasso among them—were confiscated, banned, and sometimes destroyed by Nazi officials. Such works were considered **"degenerate art,"** and were supposedly evidence of the polluting influence of Jews and Bolsheviks on European culture. The Nazis promoted, and indeed often permitted, only art forms that they believed expressed their Aryan vision of German nationalism.

Thus, Nazi Germany was in many ways a modern, industrialized, technological juggernaut. Its militarism, aggressive foreign policy, and agenda of mass murder would never have become such a terrifying force without the modern industrial power and governmental institutions that fueled the drive for global domination. But Nazism can also be viewed as a rejection of the major trends of modernization since the French Revolution. Urban society, capitalism, socialism, bourgeois culture, individualism, parliamentary politics, limited government, and modern art were all considered weak and even dangerous. This anti-modern ideology can be seen as leading directly to the Holocaust, as Hitler's regime associated the supposed evils of modern society with the Jews. Just as the Nazis popularized an imaginary, mythical vision of the heroic German people, they crafted an equally mythical vision of the Jews as the enemy of the Aryan race.

Nazi anti-Semitism was no ordinary form of bigotry or racism; it was much more vehement and thoroughgoing. Defying logic, evidence, and common sense, the Nazis claimed that the Jews were to blame for virtually everything they despised. While the German *volk* represented an agrarian ideal, to the Nazis the Jews represented an urban, modern, degenerate, and alien force. In short, since the Jews were alleged to be all that was modern, the Jews represented a "problem" for the Nazis and their mythical vision of a pure German nation. And the terrifying Final Solution to this supposed problem led to the horrors of Auschwitz and the other death camps.

QUESTION TWO

How could so many ordinary people participate in the mass murder of innocent civilians?

This is perhaps the most troubling question, and arguably the most important question raised by the Holocaust. If the Holocaust had been perpetrated by a small group of bloodthirsty or psychotic individuals, it would perhaps be easier to understand.

But the Nazis needed to mobilize the nation to carry out their atrocities, enlisting the labor of countless ordinary citizens. Can social science help us to understand this widespread brutality? Below are two approaches that might shed light on the actions of those who carried out the crimes of the Holocaust. Such approaches may not explain the root causes of the Holocaust. But they might help us to understand the sociological forces and psychological biases that may have encouraged ordinary Germans to engage in mass murder, and the psychological coping mechanisms some of them employed to endure extreme conditions.

First approach: *Psychological perspectives—justifying behaviors and coping with extremity.*

The discipline of psychology systematically examines our minds and our behaviors, and thus may offer some insight into the behaviors of those who shot, gassed, and tortured millions of innocent victims. In particular, we might examine two theories from the field of social psychology that we have studied in our fall-semester course— system justification theory and the just-world hypothesis. In addition, psychiatrist Robert Jay Lifton's theory of psychological doubling may help us understand the individual psychological strategies of Nazi doctors who carried out atrocities in concentration camps.

System justification theory suggests that we have an internal bias towards believing that the social system in which we participate is ordered and structured properly and soundly. As a result, the theory maintains, we are more likely to support the status quo than to question it. While we may see gross wealth or power inequality, racism, sexism, or other forms of oppression as objectionable, system justification theory argues that we are unlikely to question these things if they are a part of the dominant, prevailing, and **internalized** social order. Support for the status quo may help us to make sense of things by making the world seem manageable; as Jojanneke van der Toorn, et al. put it, "believing that the social system is the way it *should be* helps to reduce uncertainty and manage threat and creates a sense that there is common ground to maintain shared reality."[4]

In a similar way, according to the **just-world hypothesis,** we are likely to assume that the events that occur in the world are fair and just. The hypothesis is based on the work of social psychologist Melvin J. Lerner, who suggested that we find it psychologically comforting to assume that people get what they deserve in life. This assumption helps us to believe that the world is predictable and orderly, and that we can live our lives without fear that we will be subject to random or unfair consequences for our actions. While an underlying belief that the world is just makes sense in psychological terms, it can have troubling effects. Research on the subject of just-world hypothesis suggests that this belief may cause us to engage in **victim blaming;** for if we believe that the world is fair and just, we are likely to assume those who suffer must have done something to deserve their fate.[5]

It is perhaps not difficult to see how system justification and just-world hypothesis may help us to understand the actions of ordinary Germans during the Holocaust. If these theories are correct, it would have been psychologically difficult for both soldiers and citizens to question the prevailing order of things in Nazi Germany—in other words, to question authority and resist orders to carry out atrocities. Similarly, belief in a just world and victim blaming might make those carrying out the killings and torture believe that their actions were justified. Even though the concentration camps were filled with innocent victims, psychological tendencies may have caused the perpetrators of crimes against humanity to assume that their victims must have somehow deserved to die.

Another psychological approach to understanding the Holocaust comes from the research of Robert Jay Lifton, who studied Nazi doctors. These men provide a particularly poignant case study; as doctors, their oaths compelled them to do everything in their power to heal, and never to do harm. Yet Nazi doctors performed grotesque and deeply inhumane experiments on concentration camp victims, and oversaw mass killings in gas chambers.

Lifton suggests that doctors employed a series of psychological adaptations to maintain their sanity and ability to function in the face of their brutal acts. Among these adaptations was the development of a system of **"medicalized killing."**[6] Based on Lifton's interviews with numerous Nazi doctors, he determined that killing became medicalized in two ways. First the "controlled technology" of the gas chambers in concentration camps amounted to a "surgical" method of killing, in which the murderer was physically distanced from his victim. And second, Lifton argues that killing was medicalized in the sense that Nazi ideology maintained that it was necessary for the health of the nation; he calls this concept **"killing as a therapeutic imperative."** The Nazi worldview portrayed the Jew as a disease, a parasite, or as one Nazi doctor put it, "the gangrenous appendix in the body of mankind."[7] Therefore, according to Lifton, Nazi doctors could make sense of their work by perverting the ideals of medicine; killing Jews could be seen as "healing" the nation in the context of Nazi racial ideology.

Lifton further suggests that Nazi doctors could maintain a coherent sense of self while carrying out atrocities by engaging in a process he calls **psychological doubling.** Doubling refers to "the division of the self into two functioning wholes," whereby "one part of the self 'disavows' another part."[8] Doubling is not the same concept as multiple personality disorder, in which different personalities may exist within the same person, but as different entities in complete separation from each other. Rather, a doctor who engaged in doubling created an "Auschwitz self," capable of carrying out atrocities in the infamous concentration camp, and maintained "his prior self, in order to continue to see himself as [a] humane physician, husband, [and] father," and both selves existed in a dialectical relationship.[9] It was not as if Nazi doctors, while at home with their families, for example, did not recognize the existence of their Auschwitz selves, but rather the Auschwitz self was created by the doctor in order to transfer his conscience—it was the Auschwitz self who did the "dirty work." According to Lifton, such doubling was necessary as a means of **"adaptation to extremity,"** so that doctors could continue to function in an environment of mass murder and profound brutality.

Social psychology, then, may suggest that ordinary Germans would be oriented toward accepting existing power structures, due to system justification, and perhaps able to justify the deaths of innocent victims through just-world thinking and victim blaming. And Lifton's argument suggests that men like the Nazi doctors may have had complex psychological means of coping with extreme situations, thus making it psychologically manageable for them to engage in horrific acts. The approaches below link social psychology and sociological perspectives on the power of situational forces.

Second approach: *Sociological and Social-Psychological perspectives— role theory, the definition of the situation, obedience, and conformity.*

Sociological analysis provides insight into the ways in which we are socialized, the social forces that shape our behavior and the roles we play, and the ways in which situational forces can change our outlook and behavior. Related research in social psychology examines our tendencies toward obedience to authority and conformity to group norms. Next we will examine ways in which these perspectives might help us to understand the Holocaust.

If we wish to understand how ordinary people might be capable of extreme behavior, we might begin by turning to the **Stanford Prison Experiment,** also known as the Zimbardo Experiment. As we know from our study of Zimbardo's work in our social science course last semester, ordinary college students, with no history of violence, mental illness, or sadistic tendencies, transformed into the worst stereotypes of guard and prisoner once placed in a mock prison environment. This transformation is widely believed to be convincing evidence of the power of two concepts with which we are familiar: the **definition of the situation** and **role theory.** In a college classroom or at home, a typical college student might play the role of studious psychology major or dutiful son, respectively. But as the definition of the situation changes, and social cues and expectations change, so do roles; as a result, that student and son might begin to play the role of sadistic prison guard. As Zimbardo himself put it, the social value of his experiment "derives precisely from the fact that normal, healthy, educated young men could be so radically transformed under the institutional pressures of a 'prison environment.'"[10]

Another landmark psychological experiment that we have studied this year, which also has profound implications for the study of sociology and history, is the **Milgram Experiment.** Like Zimbardo's research, Milgram's work suggests that ordinary people are much more readily capable of engaging in disturbing, even cruel behaviors than we might like to believe. In the case of Milgram's experiment, **obedience to authority** appeared to override morality and human decency. His experiments suggest that "obedience may be a deeply ingrained behavior tendency," and thus we may follow the directives of an established authority if the definition of the situation demands it.[11] The presence of a strong authority figure, the university laboratory setting, and the resulting situational forces appear to have caused the naïve subjects in Milgram's experiment to be willing to harm other ordinary, innocent citizens.[12]

If we accept the conclusions of Zimbardo and Milgram as valid, and those conclusions are applicable beyond the narrow confines of their particular experiments, their implications for our understanding of the Holocaust are clear. The research of American historian Christopher R. Browning, supports this assumption. Browning's book, aptly titled *Ordinary Men: Reserve Police Battalion 101 and the Final Solution in Poland,* examines the role of these ordinary working-class and lower-middle class men from the city of Hamburg in Nazi atrocities. Like Zimbardo's and Milgram's subjects, the ordinary men Browning studied showed no previous inclination toward cruelty, sadism, or even any particularly pro-Nazi zeal. Yet the men of Police Battalion 101, fewer than 500 in number, killed at least 83,300 Jews.[13]

Browning points out that the not all of the men of the battalion behaved in the same way; one group among them were the most zealous killers, volunteering for the most murderous missions. A larger group proved willing to murder Jews, but did not pursue such tasks enthusiastically. And a small group, fewer than twenty per cent of the men, refused to follow kill orders or tried to evade their murderous duties. And Browning points out that "Zimbardo's spectrum of guard behavior bears an uncanny resemblance" to these patterns of behavior noted among the ordinary men of Battalion 101.[14] One might argue that, despite the widely divergent circumstances of Zimbardo's research subjects and Browning's, the dynamics of situational forces and role theory may have contributed to changes in behavior noted in both cases—ordinary people began to behave in cruel and sadistic ways.

Browning also notes connections between his research and the Milgram Experiment. As Browning notes, Milgram maintained that a high degree of obedience to authority may be expected when an individual, consciously or not, enters into an authority system that is perceived as legitimate, and then tends to "adopt the authority's perspective or 'definition of the situation.'"[15] In the case of Nazi Germany, of course, military and political officials were armed with all of the trappings of legitimate authority, and men like the soldiers of Battalion 101 existed within a hierarchical institution that valued obedience and conformity. And while Browning points out some differences between the behavior patterns of the naïve subjects of Milgram's experiment and his observations of Battalion 101, he argues that the actions he studied "render considerable support to [Milgram's] conclusions, and some of his observations are clearly confirmed."[16]

For example, like Milgram's subjects, the men of the police battalion were less likely to be obedient when they were in close proximity to the suffering of their victims. Greater distance, on the other hand, allowed them to feel less connected to their assigned tasks, and therefore made them more likely to obey orders to harm victims. In addition, like the behavior of Milgram's subjects when they were not directly monitored by authority, "many policemen did not comply with orders when not directly supervised."[17] Browning's study clearly makes the case for the definition of the situation, role theory, and Milgram's analysis of obedience dynamics in his study of ordinary men who carried out extraordinary crimes.

Browning also argues that additional factors appear to have contributed to the actions of the policemen he studied. Years of vehement and widespread anti-Semitic propaganda, for example, had prepared the men to accept the idea that Jews were a problem that needed to be addressed. He also points to another topic we addressed in our study of social psychology last semester—**conformity.** As the **Asch Experiments** of the 1950s suggest, humans seem to have a surprisingly strong tendency to conform to the behaviors of the majority around us. Solomon Asch tested this tendency by asking subjects to pick matching sets of lines from a group; while the answer was quite visibly obvious, a high number of the subjects gave the wrong answer when a majority around them (who were cooperating with Asch's experiment) intentionally gave the wrong answer. Browning's analysis of Police Battalion 101 suggests that the tendency to conform also exists in much more serious circumstances than picking lines from a sheet of paper. He maintains that between eighty and ninety per cent of the policemen killed innocent victims, even though they were initially horrified by the idea, as "[t]o break ranks and step out, to adopt overtly nonconformist behavior, was simply beyond most of the men. It was easier for them to shoot."[18]

The findings of classical psychological experiments by Philip Zimbardo, Stanley Milgram, and Solomon Asch, then, may give us some insight into the actions of ordinary Germans who perpetrated the crimes of the Holocaust. The power of situational forces and role theory may also help us to understand the actions of those who, while showing no previous inclination toward violence or sadism, participated in the mass murder of innocents.

Some Concluding Thoughts

The approaches to understanding the Holocaust examined above are by no means the only ways to analyze or understand it, and many more questions are raised by this horrifying event than can possibly be addressed in any single article, book, or university course. And, crucially, none of the approaches to understanding the Holocaust examined above can justify the atrocities of Auschwitz or any of the other brutal crimes of oppression, torture, and murder that took place at the direction of Nazi leadership. No historical, psychological, or sociological theory or insight can possibly excuse acts of grave inhumanity. To seek to understand the Holocaust is not the same as trying to "explain it away" or detract from its significance. Quite the opposite is true. We must study the Holocaust because of its important place in our history as human beings, and because of its brutal nature. We must seek to understand horrifying events like the Holocaust in order to learn something from them, to try to prevent them from occurring again. The twisted vision of Adolf Hitler may be dismissed as the product of a brutal madman's mind, from which we might learn little. But the Holocaust occurred because of the actions of a whole society. It demands our attention and our best effort to learn from it. We start this process, as grim as it may be, by *thinking* about it.

Notes

1. The full text on the signs reads as follows: "THE NEXT TIME YOU SEE INJUSTICE, THE NEXT TIME YOU WITNESS HATRED, THE NEXT TIME YOU HEAR ABOUT GENOCIDE, THINK ABOUT WHAT YOU SAW."

2. See Max Weber, "On Bureaucracy," in *Readings in Social Theory and Modernization*, ed. John McGrath (Boston: Pearson, 2011).

3. Zygmunt Bauman, *Modernity and the Holocaust* (Ithaca, NY: Cornell University Press, 2000), 17.

4. Jojanneke van der Toorn, Tom R. Tyler, and John T. Jost, "More than fair: Outcome dependence, system justification, and the perceived legitimacy of authority figures," *Journal of Experimental Social Psychology* 47 (2011) 128.

5. See Melvin J. Lerner, *Belief in a Just World: A Fundamental Delusion* (New York: Plenum Press, 1980).

6. Robert Jay Lifton, "The Nazi Doctors," in *The Holocaust,* ed. Donald Niewyk (Boston: Houghton Mifflin, 2003), 60.

7. Ibid., 61–62.

8. Ibid., 66.

9. Ibid., 65.

10. Philip G. Zimbardo, W. Curtis Banks, Craig Haney, and David Jaffey, "The Mind is a Formidable Jailer," in *Readings in Social Theory and Modernization,* ed. John McGrath (Boston: Pearson, 2011), 66.

11. Stanley Milgram, "The Dilemma of Obedience," in *Readings in Social Theory and Modernization,* ed. John McGrath (Boston: Pearson, 2011), 50.

12. The "learners" in Milgram's experiment, of course, were not actually being shocked, as they were complicit with the researcher in the experiment. But as far as the naïve "teachers" knew, they were administering powerful electric shocks to the learners.

13. Christopher R. Browning, "Ordinary Men," in *The Holocaust,* ed. Donald Niewyk (Boston: Houghton Mifflin, 2003), 80.

14. Ibid., 82.

15. Ibid., 83.

16. Ibid., 85.

17. Ibid.

18. Ibid., 87.

Concerning Violence

Frantz Fanon

Frantz Fanon (1925–1961), a French-educated psychiatrist from Martinique, was an active supporter of the Algerian independence struggle. He received international recognition after World War Two for his leadership in the global anticolonialist movement.

National liberation, national renaissance, the restoration of nationhood to the people, commonwealth: whatever maybe the headings used or the new formulas introduced, decolonization is always a violent phenomenon. At whatever level we study it—relationships between individuals, new names for sports clubs, the human admixture at cocktail parties, in the police, on the directing boards of national or private banks—decolonization is quite simply the replacing of a certain "species" of men by another "species" of men. Without any period of transition, there is a total, complete, and absolute substitution. It is true that we could equally well stress the rise of a new nation, the setting up of a new state, its diplomatic relations, and its economic and political trends. But we have precisely chosen to speak of that kind of tabula rasa which characterizes at the outset all decolonization. Its unusual importance is that it constitutes, from the very first day, the minimum demands of the colonized. To tell the truth, the proof of success lies in a whole social structure being changed from the bottom up. The extraordinary importance of this change is that it is willed, called for, demanded. The need for this change exists in its crude state, impetuous and compelling, in the consciousness and in the lives of the men and women who are colonized. But the possibility of this change is equally experienced in the form of a terrifying future in the consciousness of another "species" of men and women: the colonizers.

Decolonization, which sets out to change the order of the world, is, obviously, a program of complete disorder. But it cannot come as a result of magical practices, nor of a natural shock, nor of a friendly understanding. Decolonization, as we know, is a historical process: that is to say that it cannot be understood, it cannot become intelligible nor clear to itself except in the exact measure that we can discern the movements which give it historical form and content. Decolonization is the meeting of two forces, opposed to each other by their very nature, which in fact owe their originality to that sort of substantification which results from and is nourished by the situation in the colonies. Their first encounter was marked by violence and their existence together—that is to say the exploitation of the native by the settler—was carried on by dint of a great array of bayonets and cannons. The settler and the native are old acquaintances. In fact, the settler is right when he speaks of knowing "them" well. For it is the settler who has brought the native into existence and who perpetuates his existence. The settler owes the fact of his very existence, that is to say, his property, to the colonial system.

Decolonization never takes place unnoticed, for it influences individuals and modifies them fundamentally. It transforms spectators crushed with their inessentiality into privileged actors, with the grandiose glare of history's floodlights upon them. It brings a natural rhythm into existence, introduced by new men, and with it a new language and a new humanity. Decolonization is the veritable creation of new men. But this creation owes nothing of its legitimacy to any supernatural power; the "thing" which has been colonized becomes man during the same process by which it frees itself.

In decolonization, there is therefore the need of a complete calling in question of the colonial situation. If we wish to describe it precisely, we might find it in the well-known words: "The last shall be first and the first last." Decolonization is the putting into practice of this sentence. That is why, if we try to describe it, all decolonization is successful.

The naked truth of decolonization evokes for us the searing bullets and blood-stained knives which emanate from it. For if the last shall be first, this will only come to pass after a murderous and decisive struggle between the two protagonists. That affirmed intention to place the last at the head of things, and to make them climb at a pace (too quickly, some say) the well-known steps which characterize an organized society, can only triumph if we use all means to turn the scale, including, of course, that of violence.

You do not turn any society, however primitive it may be, upside down with such a program if you have not decided from the very beginning, that is to say from the actual formulation of that program, to overcome all the obstacles that you will come across in so doing. The native who decides to put the program into practice, and to become its moving force, is ready for violence at all times. From birth it is clear to him that this narrow world, strewn with prohibitions, can only be called in question by absolute violence.

The colonial world is a world divided into compartments. It is probably unnecessary to recall the existence of native quarters and European quarters, of schools for natives and schools for Europeans; in the same way we need not recall apartheid in South Africa. Yet, if we examine closely this system of compartments, we will at least be able to reveal the lines of force it implies. This approach to the colonial world, its ordering and its geographical layout will allow us to mark out the lines on which a decolonized society will be reorganized.

The colonial world is a world cut in two. The dividing line, the frontiers are shown by barracks and police stations. In the colonies it is the policeman and the soldier who are the official, instituted go-betweens, the spokesmen of the settler and his rule of oppression. In capitalist societies the educational system, whether lay or clerical, the structure of moral reflexes handed down from father to son, the exemplary honesty of workers who are given a medal after fifty years of good and loyal service, and the affection which springs from harmonious relations and good behavior—all these aesthetic expressions of respect for the established order serve to create around the exploited person an atmosphere of submission and of inhibition which lightens the task of policing considerably. In the capitalist countries a multitude of moral teachers, counselors and "bewilderers" separate the exploited from those in power. In the colonial countries, on the contrary, the policeman and the soldier, by their immediate presence and their frequent and direct action maintain contact with the native and advise him by means of rifle butts and napalm not to budge. It is obvious here that the agents of government speak the language of pure force. The intermediary does not lighten the oppression, nor seek to hide the domination; he shows them up and puts them into practice with the clear conscience of an upholder of the peace; yet he is the bringer of violence into the home and into the mind of the native.

The zone where the natives live is not complementary to the zone inhabited by the settlers. The two zones are opposed, but not in the service of a higher unity. Obedient to the rules of pure Aristotelian logic, they both follow the principle of reciprocal exclusivity. No conciliation is possible, for of the two terms, one is superfluous. The settlers' town is a strongly built town; all made of stone and steel. It is a brightly lit town; the streets are covered with asphalt, and the garbage cans swallow all the leavings, unseen, unknown and hardly thought about. The settler's feet are never visible, except perhaps in the sea; but there you're never close enough to see them. His feet are protected by strong shoes although the streets of his town are clean and even, with no holes or stones. The settler's town is a well-fed town, an easygoing town; its belly is always full of good things. The settlers' town is a town of white people, of foreigners.

The town belonging to the colonized people, or at least the native town, the Negro village, the medina, the reservation, is a place of ill fame, peopled by men of evil repute. They are born there, it matters little where or how; they die there, it matters not where, nor how. It is a world without spaciousness; men live there on top of each other, and their huts are built one on top of the other. The native town is a hungry town, starved of bread, of meat, of shoes, of coal, of light. The native town is a crouching village, a town on its knees, a town wallowing in the mire. It is a town of niggers and dirty Arabs. The look that the native turns on the settler's town is a look of lust, a look of envy; it expresses his dreams of possession—all manner of possession: to sit at the settler's table, to sleep in the settler's bed, with his wife if possible. The colonized man is an envious man. And this the settler knows very well; when their glances meet he ascertains bitterly, always on the defensive, "They want to take our place." It is true, for there is no native who does not dream at least once a day of setting himself up in the settler's place.

This world divided into compartments, this world cut in two is inhabited by two different species. The originality of the colonial context is that economic reality, inequality, and the immense difference of ways of life never come to mask the human realities. When you examine at close quarters the colonial context, it is evident that what parcels out the world is to begin with the fact of belonging to or not belonging to a given race, a given species. In the colonies the economic substructure is also a superstructure. The cause is the consequence; you are rich because you are white, you are white because you are rich. This is why Marxist analysis should always be slightly stretched every time we have to do with the colonial problem.

Everything up to and including the very nature of pre-capitalist society, so well explained by Marx, must here be thought out again. The serf is in essence different from the knight, but a reference to divine right is necessary to legitimize this statutory difference. In the colonies, the foreigner coming from another country imposed his rule by means of guns and machines. In defiance of his successful transplantation, in spite of his appropriation, the settler still remains a foreigner. It is neither the act of owning factories, nor estates, nor a bank balance which distinguishes the governing classes. The governing race is first and foremost those who come from elsewhere, those who are unlike the original inhabitants, "the others."

The violence which has ruled over the ordering of the colonial world, which has ceaselessly drummed the rhythm for the destruction of native social forms and broken up without reserve the systems of reference of the economy, the customs of dress and external life, that same violence will be claimed and taken over by the native at the moment when, deciding to embody history in his own person, he surges into the forbidden quarters. To wreck the colonial world is henceforward a mental picture of action which is very clear, very easy to understand and which may be assumed by each one of the individuals which constitute the colonized people. To break up the colonial world does not mean that after the frontiers have been abolished lines of communication will be set up between the two zones. The destruction of the colonial world is no more and no less that the abolition of one zone, its burial in the depths of the earth or its expulsion from the county.

Nonviolent Power in Action

Introduction

Real swaraj *[freedom] is self-rule or self-control. The way to it is* satyagraha: *the power of truth and love . . .*

In my opinion, we have used the term "swaraj" without understanding its real significance. I have endeavoured to explain it as I understand it, and my conscience testifies that my life henceforth is dedicated to its attainment.
> —*M.K. Gandhi,* Hind Swaraj, *1909*[1]

Mohandas Karamchand Gandhi (1869–1948) was called "Mahatma" ("Great Soul") because of his extraordinary achievements as leader of the Indian movement for independence. Gandhi was not primarily a theorist but a reformer and activist. When pressed for a treatise on his philosophy, he protested that "I am not built for academic writings. Action is my domain."[2] Yet he was guided by values and ideas that remained remarkably enduring throughout his life. Chief among them were his unique concepts of freedom and power, or, to use his terms, of swaraj and satyagraha. As seen from his statement quoted above, these were closely connected ideas, related to each other as means to end. He did, as he promised in 1909, devote his life to the pursuit of swaraj and he redefined the concept by insisting that individual freedom and social responsibility were no more antithetical than self-realization and self-restraint. In his pursuit of freedom he transformed our conception of power through his practice of nonviolence and satyagraha. Today the Mahatma has come to mean innumerable things to multitudes around the world. At least one of his important achievements was to show how the use of nonviolent power may clarify and enlarge our understanding of freedom.

Freedom as Swaraj: Redefinitions

In the heat of India's struggle for independence from British rule, the goal of swaraj was constantly invoked. It often meant simply freedom for India. But Gandhi argued that the word should mean more than political independence. When in 1931 he was asked to define the term precisely, he said it was not easily translated into a single

English word. But he then went on to explain its meaning as it had evolved since the beginning of the nationalist movement:

> [According to Gandhi,] The root meaning of *swaraj* is self-rule. *Swaraj* may, therefore, be rendered as disciplined rule from within. . . . 'Independence' has no such limitation. Independence may mean license to do as you like. *Swaraj* is positive. Independence is negative. . . . The word *swaraj* is a sacred word, a Vedic word, meaning self-rule and self-restraint, and not freedom from all restraint which 'independence' often means.[3]

When Gandhi invoked ancient Vedic tradition in this way to define swaraj, he knew that it would allow for interpreting the idea of freedom in two distinct senses. Swaraj meant literally "self-rule" and could denote, in a strict political sense, a sovereign kingdom's freedom from external control.[4] Or it could mean freedom in a spiritual sense as being free from illusion and ignorance. From this perspective, one is liberated as one gains greater self-knowledge and consequent self-mastery. Obsessions with money or other means of domination become addictive forms of human bondage; freedom comes as we learn through self-discipline to rule ourselves. Thus, *The Bhagavad-Gita,* Gandhi's primary text of Hinduism, saw the liberated individual as one who "acts without craving, possessiveness," and "finds peace" in awareness of the "infinite spirit," thereby being "freed from delusion."[5] The *Chandogya Upanishad,* like the *Gita,* defined freedom in a spiritual sense: "self-governing autonomy" and "unlimited freedom in all worlds," were the traits of swaraj in the sage. As in the *Gita,* this liberation evolved from a higher consciousness, an awareness of the unity of all being, the identity of oneself with the universal Self or *Atman.*[6]

The last point that Gandhi developed in his theory of swaraj was his insistence that social reforms were essential for India's freedom. When he asserted that "the movement for *Swaraj* is a movement for self-purification,"[7] he meant that individuals must take responsibility for a change of attitude to overcome three major problems in Indian society: Hindu-Muslim religious conflict, the evils of caste and untouchability, and economic inequality. Each of these areas of social corruption was an obstacle to swaraj and must be tackled coterminously with the fight for political independence.[8] "The sooner it is recognized" he said, "that many of our social evils impede our march towards *Swaraj,* the greater will be our progress towards our cherished goal. To postpone social reform till after the attainment of *Swaraj* is not to know the meaning of *Swaraj.*"[9]

Satyagraha as a Form of Power

William Shirer went to India in 1930 as an American journalist to report on what he then saw as Gandhi's "peculiar revolution." Fifty years later he wrote a remarkable memoir about that visit. He described the civil disobedience campaign of that year in compelling terms and then concluded that satyagraha was Gandhi's "supreme achievement," which "taught us all that there was a greater power in life than force, which seemed to have ruled the planet since men first sprouted on it. That power lay in the spirit, in Truth and Love, in non-violent action."[10] Whether or not Gandhi in fact "taught us all" this lesson, the phenomenon of the power of satyagraha is there for all to know. And whether or not one accepts that this power derived from "Truth and love," the Indian independence movement remains one of the largest mobilizations of mass energy in history; it did exercise a form of power dramatically different from that of governments or armies or violent revolutions. This was because its leadership conceived of how to convert the power of nonviolence into political action.

Gandhi defined satyagraha as the power "born of Truth and Love or non-violence."[11] As early as 1909, he presented it as his method for attaining swaraj. He believed, on the basis of his use of civil disobedience in South Africa from 1906 to 1914, that the power of nonviolent action identified with satyagraha was uniquely suited for achieving the "inward" as well as the "outward" freedom of swaraj. The word satyagraha was coined by Gandhi by joining the Sanskrit *satya* (truth) with *agraha* (holding firmly)[12] and the historical context of this derivation will be traced in the next chapter. He drew a sharp distinction between satyagraha and "passive resistance" because the latter allowed for "internal violence," the harboring of enmity and anger among resisters even when they commit no physical violence. Gandhi asserted that unlike passive resistance, "Satyagraha is gentle, it never wounds. It must not be the result of anger or malice."[13]

Much depends on the intent or motive of the *satyagrahi* (practitioner of satyagraha). Wrong motives occur when the intent is only to attain victory or satisfaction of a selfish interest. A *satyagrahi* concentrates on the common interest and strives not for retribution but to transform a conflict situation so that warring parties can come out of a confrontation convinced that it was in their mutual interest to resolve it. This was not unlike the scene in 1947 when without mutual recrimination the British left India after centuries of colonization.

Gandhi's conceptions of swaraj and satyagraha were both related to the emphasis that he placed on employing the right means to attain an end. This was another of the key ideas that he had expressed in *Hind Swaraj*. He argued there that: "the belief that there is no connection between the means and the end is a great mistake. Through that mistake even men who have been considered religious have committed grievous crimes.... The means may be likened to a seed, the end to a tree; and there is just the same inviolable connection between the means and the end as there is between the seed and the tree.... We reap exactly as we sow."[14]

Thus Gandhi can say that "Means and ends are convertible terms in my philosophy of life."[15] When it was rumored in late 1924 that he would be invited by the Soviet government to visit the USSR, he replied that he had been courted by Communists before, and reflected unfavorably on the Russian revolution:

> I do not believe in short-violent-cuts to success. Those Bolshevik friends who are bestowing their attention on me should realize that however much I may sympathize with and admire worthy motives, I am an uncompromising opponent of violent methods even to serve the noblest of causes. There is, therefore, really no meeting ground between the school of violence and myself.[16]

Whenever he considered the kind of revolution that India needed, he stressed this emphasis on means as the basis of swaraj and satyagraha. As he planned the mass civil disobedience campaign that would be called the salt satyagraha, he went before the Indian people to argue his case in these terms:

> No one will be able to stand in our way when we have developed the strength to win *swaraj*. Everyone's freedom is within his grasp. There are two alternatives before us. The one is that of violence, the other of non-violence; the one of physical strength, the other of soul-force; the one of hatred, the other love . . . If we want *swaraj*, we shall have to strive hard and follow one of these two courses. As they are incompatible with each other, the fruit, the *swaraj* that would be secured by following the one would necessarily be different from that which would be secured by following the other. . . . We reap as we sow.[17]

When Gandhi assumed leadership of the nationalist movement in 1919 he described satyagraha in terms of a metaphor that likened it to "a banyan tree with innumerable branches." The trunk of the tree, he said, consisted not only of nonviolence (*ahimsa*) but also of truth (*satya*).[18] So the last component of satyagraha to be introduced here is Gandhi's concept of truth. He begins with a warning to each of us: we must continually remind ourselves of our fallibility by recognizing our limitations. Human understanding is always imperfect and thus incapable of possessing absolute truth.[19] We may believe in truth or in God, or, as Gandhi did, in Truth as God. But we cannot possess complete knowledge of either and "the claim to infallibility would always be a most dangerous claim to make."[20]

Nonviolence therefore becomes imperative in any human conflict because there are inevitably partial and contending perceptions of truth. Leaders of nations are notorious for their claims to carry truth as they lead their people into battle. Gandhi offered his method to the world as a corrective: "*Satyagraha* . . . excludes the use of violence because man is not capable of knowing the absolute truth and, therefore, not competent to punish."[21] When Gandhi was questioned in 1920 by a Government tribunal about the volatile nature of civil disobedience, a British official asked: "However honestly a man may strive in his search for truth his notions of truth will be different" and would this not produce violent disorder? Gandhi replied that was precisely the reason why "non-violence was the necessary corollary," because without this India could not gain swaraj.[22] This answer hardly satisfied the British government in 1920. But it did underscore the integral relationship that Gandhi drew between truth and nonviolence. These remained the two overriding values that directed his quest for personal and political liberation. He usually spoke of truth in terms of a search: "Truth resides in every human heart, and one has to search for it there, and to be guided by truth as one sees it. But no one has a right to coerce others to act according to his own view of truth."[23] The essence of Gandhi's optimism about each person's pursuit of truth or of self-realization is here; equally significant is how nonviolence may be interpreted as both a guiding value and a warning, that we have no right to violate others.

Notes

1. M. K. Gandhi, *The Collected Works of Mahatma Gandhi* [hereafter, *CWMG*], Publications Division, Ministry of Information and Broadcasting, Government of India, 1961, 10, p. 64; and M. K. Gandhi, *Hind Swarajya* (Ahmedabad, Navijivan, Prakashan Mandir Publishing House), 1979, p. 269–271. The latter is a photostatic copy of Gandhi's original handwritten text in Gujarati. The present author is indebted to Pyarelal Nayar, D. G. Dave, and Sita N. Kapadia for their assistance in translating and interpreting the Gujarati text, and for the former's interpretation of satyagraha as "power." Although Gandhi himself translated satyagraha as "truth-force," it is suggested here that "power" is a preferable translation because "force" is often associated with violence. The specific identification of satyagraha as a form of power accords with the valuable analysis of power in Gene Sharp, *The Politics of Nonviolent Action* (Boston: Porter Sargent, 1973), pp. 3–48. See Gandhi's discussion of power in Pyarelal, *Mahatma Gandhi: The Last Phase,* vol. 2 (Ahmedabad: Navajivan, 1958), pp. 630–633.

2. *CWMG* 83: 180

3. *CWMG* 45: 263–264.

4. The Sanskrit pronoun *sva* means "own, one's own, my own, or self." (Sir M. Monier-Williams, *A Sanskrit-English Dictionary,* New Edition, Oxford, Clarendon, 1899, pp. 1275–1276). Thus *sva-raj* as used in Vedic texts signified "self-ruling," "self-ruler," one's own rule. *Sva* becomes *swa* with most modern Indian writers, with *svarajya* (self-rule) as the Sanskrit substantive. The *Rig Veda* and *Atharvaveda* used *svaraj* in the political sense of "self-ruler" and usually "king." This kingship could be either divine or terrestrial, applying to Indra, "king" of the gods, or occasionally to earthly kings of western India. (A. A. MacDonell and A. B. Keith, *Vedic Index of Names and Subjects* (London, John Murray, 1912), 2: 494; *Aitareya Brahmana* VIII. 14. in MacDonell and Keith, ibid., p. 494. For complete reference see *Rigveda Brahmanas, The Aitareya and Kausitaki Brahmanas of the Rig-Veda,* translated by A. B. Keith, Harvard Oriental Series, 30 volumes (Cambridge: Harvard University Press, 1920), 25: 330.

5. *The Bhagavad-Gita,* 2: 71–72, translated by Barbara Stoler Miller (New York: Bantam, 1986), p. 39. The meaning of freedom in this sense need not exclude kings or political leaders because they may possess also the spiritual qualities of self-rule. Barbara Miller examines the idea of the "royal sage," a leader of spiritual power and knowledge in *Theater of Memory* (New York: Columbia University Press, 1984), pp. 8–9.

6. *Chandogya Upanishad,* VII, 25, 2, in *The Principal Upanishads,* edited by S. Radhakrishnan (London: George Allen and Unwin, 1969), p. 488. Those who do not possess knowledge of self and of the universal Self "have no freedom" and are "subject to others (*anya-raj*)." This concept

of spiritual freedom may be compared and contrasted with the idea expressed in Christ's maxim, "And ye shall know the truth and the truth shall make you free." St. John. 8:32.

7. *CWMG* 24: 227.

8. *CWMG* 75: 158.

9. *CWMG* 36: 470.

10. William Shirer, *Gandhi: A Memoir.* (New York: Simon and Schuster, 1979) p. 245.

11. *CWMG* 29: 92.

12. Bhikhu Parekh argues that *agraha* was used by Gandhi "in its ordinary Gujarati and not the classical Sanskrit sense, [that] means insisting on something without becoming obstinate or uncompromising" which then denotes "both insistence on and for truth." *Gandhi's Political Philosophy* (Indiana: University of Notre Dame Press, 1989), p. 143. These two connotations from Gujarati and Sanskrit are complementary and Parekh's point highlights the distinction that Gandhi made between passive resistance (or *duragraha*) and *satyagraha*: the former in Gandhi's view was "obstinate or uncompromising."

13. *CWMG* 54: 416.

14. *CWMG* 10: 431. Analysts of Gandhi's thought have focused on the centrality of his theory of means. Joan Bondurant devotes careful attention to this in *Conquest of Violence* (Princeton: Princeton University Press, 1988), especially chapter 7, pp. 189–233, which begins "The challenge of Gandhian *satyagraha* centers upon the necessity of reconciling ends and means through a philosophy of action." Raghavan Iyer offers a cogent analysis of the subject in *The Moral and Political Thought of Mahatma Gandhi*, chapter 13, arguing that "Gandhi seems to stand almost alone among social and political thinkers in his firm rejection of the rigid dichotomy between ends and means and in his extreme preoccupation with the means to the extent that they, rather than the ends, provide the standard of reference" (p. 361).

15. *CWMG* 25: 480.

16. *CWMG* 25: 424.

17. *CWMG* 37: 250–251.

18. *CWMG* 15: 244.

19. *CWMG* 21: 457.

20. *CWMG* 33: 247.

21. *CWMG* 19: 466.

22. *CWMG* 16: 409.

23. *CWMG* 46: 216.

Why Can't People Feed Themselves?

Frances Moore Lappé and Joseph Collins

Question: You have said that the hunger problem is not the result of over-population. But you have not answered the most basic and simple question of all: Why can't people feed themselves? As Senator Daniel P. Moynihan put it bluntly, when addressing himself to the Third World, "Food growing is the first thing you do when you come down out of the trees. The question is, how come the United States can grow food and you can't?"

Our Response: In the very first speech I, Frances, ever gave after writing Diet for a Small Planet, I tried to take my audience along the path that I had taken in attempting to understand why so many are hungry in this world. Here is the gist of that talk that was, in truth, a turning point in my life:

When I started I saw a world divided into two parts: a minority of nations that had "taken off" through their agricultural and industrial revolutions to reach a level of unparalleled material abundance and a majority that remained behind in a primitive, traditional, undeveloped state. This lagging behind of the majority of the world's peoples must be due, I thought, to some internal deficiency or even to several of them. It seemed obvious that the underdeveloped countries must be deficient in natural resources—particularly good land and climate—and in cultural development, including modern attitudes conducive to work and progress.

But when looking for the historical roots of the predicament, I learned that my picture of these two separate worlds was quite false. My "two separate worlds" were really just different sides of the same coin. One side was on top largely because the other side was on the bottom. Could this be true? How were these separate worlds related?

Colonialism appeared to me to be the link. Colonialism destroyed the cultural patterns of production and exchange by which traditional societies in "underdeveloped" countries previously had met the needs of the people. Many precolonial social structures, while dominated by exploitative elites, had evolved a system of mutual obligations among the classes that helped to ensure at least a minimal diet for all. A friend of mine once said: "Precolonial village existence in subsistence agriculture was a limited life indeed, but its certainly not Calcutta." The misery of starvation in the streets of Calcutta can only be understood as the end-point of a long historical process—one that has destroyed a traditional social system.

"Underdeveloped," instead of being an adjective that evokes the picture of a static society, became for me a verb (to "underdevelop") meaning the *process* by which the minority of the world has transformed—indeed often robbed and degraded—the majority.

That was in 1972. I clearly recall my thoughts on my return home. I had stated publicly for the first time a world view that had taken me years of study to grasp. The sense of relief was tremendous. For me the breakthrough lay in realizing that today's "hunger crisis" could not be described in static, descriptive terms. Hunger and underdevelopment must always be thought of as a *process*.

To answer the question "why hunger?" it is counterproductive to simply *describe* the conditions in an underdeveloped country today. For these conditions, whether they be the degree of malnutrition, the levels of agricultural production, or even the country's ecological endowment, are not static factors—they are not "givens." They are rather the *results* of an ongoing historical process. As we dug ever deeper into that historical process for the preparation of this book, we began to discover the existence of scarcity-creating mechanisms that we had only vaguely intuited before.

We have gotten great satisfaction from probing into the past since we recognized it is the only way to approach a solution to hunger today. We have come to see that it is the *force* creating the condition, not the condition itself, that must be the target of change. Otherwise we might change the condition today, only to find tomorrow that it has been recreated—with a vengeance.

Asking the question "Why can't people feed themselves?" carries a sense of bewilderment that there are so many people in the world not able to feed themselves adequately. What astonished us, however, is that there are not more people in the world who are hungry—considering the weight of the centuries of effort by the few to undermine the capacity of the majority to feed themselves. No, we are not crying "conspiracy!" If these forces were entirely conspiratorial, they would be easier to detect and many more people would by now have risen up to resist. We are talking about something more subtle and insidious; a heritage of colonial order in which people with the advantage of considerable power sought their own self-interest, often arrogantly believing they were acting in the interest of the people whose lives they were destroying.

The Colonial Mind

The colonizer viewed agriculture in the subjugated lands as primitive and backward. Yet such a view contrasts sharply with the documents from the colonial period now coming to light. For example, A. J. Voelker, a British agricultural scientist assigned to India during the 1890s, wrote:

Nowhere would one find better instances of keeping land scrupulously clean from weeds, of ingenuity in device of water-raising appliances, of knowledge of soils and their capabilities, as well as of the exact time to sow and reap, as one would find in Indian agriculture. It is wonderful, too, how much is known of rotation, the system of "mixed crops" and of fallowing.

. . . I, at least, have never seen a more perfect picture of cultivation."[1]

None the less, viewing the agriculture of the vanquished as primitive and backward reinforced the colonizer's rationale for destroying it. To the colonizers of Africa, Asia, and Latin America, agriculture became merely a means to extract wealth—much as gold from a mine—on behalf of the colonizing power. Agriculture was no longer seen as a source of food for the local population, nor even as their livelihood. Indeed the English economist John Stuart Mill reasoned that colonies should not be thought of as civilizations or countries at all but as "agricultural establishments" whose sole purpose was to supply the "larger community to which they belong." The colonized society's agriculture was only a subdivision of the agricultural system of the metropolitan country. As Mill acknowledged, "Our West India colonies, for example, cannot be regarded as countries . . . The West Indies are the place where England *finds it convenient* to carry on the production of sugar, coffee and a few other tropical commodities."[2]

Prior to European intervention, Africans practiced a diversified agriculture that included the introduction of new food plants of Asian or American origin. But colonial rule simplified this diversified production to single cash crops—often to the exclusion of staple foods—and in the process sowed the seeds of famine.[3]

Rice farming once had been common in Gambia. But with colonial rule so much of the best land was taken over by peanuts (grown for the European market) that rice had to be imported to counter the mounting prospect of famine. Northern Ghana, once famous for its yams and other foodstuffs, was forced to concentrate solely on cocoa. Most of the Gold Coast thus became dependent on cocoa. Liberia was turned into a virtual plantation subsidiary of Firestone Tire and Rubber. Food production in Dahomey and southeast Nigeria was all but abandoned in favor of palm oil; Tanganyika (now Tanzania) was forced to focus on sisal and Uganda on cotton.

The same happened in Indochina. About the time of the American Civil War the French decided that the Mekong Delta in Vietnam would be ideal for producing rice for export. Through a production system based on enriching the large landowners, Vietnam became the world's third largest exporter of rice by the 1930s; yet many landless Vietnamese went hungry.[4]

Rather than helping the peasants, colonialism's public works programs only reinforced export crop production. British irrigation works built in nineteenth-century India did help increase production, but the expansion was for spring export crops at the expense of millets and legumes grown in the fall as the basic local food crops.

Because people living on the land do not easily go against their natural and adaptive drive to grow food for themselves, colonial powers had to force the production of cash crops. The first strategy was to use physical or economic force to get the local population to grow cash crops instead of food on their own plots and then turn them over to the colonizer for export. The second strategy was the direct takeover of the land by large-scale plantations growing crops for export.

Forced Peasant Production

As Walter Rodney recounts in *How Europe Underdeveloped Africa*, cash crops were often grown literally under threat of guns and whips.[5] One visitor to the Sahel commented in 1928: "Cotton is an artificial crop and one the value of which is not entirely clear to the natives. . ." He wryly noted the "enforced enthusiasm with which the natives . . . have thrown themselves into . . . planting cotton."[6] The forced cultivation of cotton was a major grievance leading to the Maji Maji wars in Tanzania (then Tanganyika) and behind the nationalist revolt in Angola as late as 1960.[7]

Although raw force was used, taxation was the preferred colonial technique to force Africans to grow cash crops. The colonial administrations simply levied taxes on cattle, land, houses, and even the people themselves. Since the tax had to be paid in the coin of the realm, the peasants had either to grow crops to sell or to work on the plantations or in the mines of the Europeans.[8] Taxation was both an effective tool to "stimulate" cash cropping and a source of revenue that the colonial bureaucracy needed to enforce the system. To expand their production of export crops to pay the mounting taxes, peasant producers were forced to neglect the farming of food crops. In 1830, the Dutch administration in Java made the peasants an offer they could not refuse; if they would grow government-owned export crops on one fifth of their land, the Dutch would remit their land taxes.[9] If they refused and thus could not pay the taxes, they lost their land.

Marketing boards emerged in Africa in the 1930s as another technique for getting the profit from cash crop production by native producers into the hands of the colonial government and international firms. Purchases by the marketing boards were well below the world market price. Peanuts bought by the boards from peasant cultivators in West Africa were sold in Britain for more than *seven times* what the peasants received.[10]

The marketing board concept was born with the "cocoa hold-up" in the Gold Coast in 1937. Small cocoa farmers refused to sell to the large cocoa concerns like United Africa Company (a subsidiary Anglo-Dutch firm, Unilever—which we know as Lever Brothers) and Cadbury until they got a higher price. When the British government stepped in and agreed to buy the cocoa directly in place of the big business concerns, the smallholders must have thought they had scored atleast a minor victory. But had they really? The following year the British formally set up the West African Cocoa Control Board. Theoretically, its purpose was to pay the peasants a reasonable price for their crops. In practice, however, the board, as sole purchaser, was able hold down the prices paid the peasants for their crops when the world prices were rising. Rodney sums up the real "victory":

> None of the benefits went to Africans, but rather to the British government itself and to the private companies . . . Big companies like the United African Company and John Holt were given . . . quotas to fulfill on behalf of the boards. As agents of the government, they were no longer exposed to direct attack, and their profits were secure.[11]

These marketing boards, set up for most export crops, were actually controlled by the companies. The chairman of the Cocoa Board was none other than John Cadbury of Cadbury Brothers (ever had a Cadbury chocolate bar?) who was part of a buying pool exploiting West African cocoa farmers.

The marketing boards funneled part of the profits from the exploitation of peasant producers indirectly into the royal treasury. While the Cocoa Board sold to the British Food Ministry at low prices, the ministry upped the price for British manufacturers, thus netting a profit as high as 11 million pounds in some years.[12]

These marketing boards of Africa were only the institutionalized rendition of what is the essence of colonialism—the extraction of wealth. While profits continued to accrue to foreign interests and local elites, prices received by those actually growing the commodities remained low.

Plantations

A second approach was direct takeover of the land either by the colonizing government or by private foreign interests. Previously self-provisioning farmers were forced to cultivate the plantation fields through either enslavement or economic coercion.

After the conquest of the Kandyan Kingdom (in present day Sri Lanka), in 1815, the British designated all the vast central part of the island as crown land. When it was determined that coffee, a profitable export crop, could be grown there, the Kandyan lands were sold off to British investors and planters at a mere five shillings per acre, the government even defraying the cost of surveying and road building.[13]

Java is also a prime example of a colonial government seizing territory and then putting it into private foreign hands. In 1870, the Dutch declared all uncultivated land—called waste land—property of the state for lease to Dutch plantation enterprises. In addition, the Agrarian Land Law of 1870 authorized foreign companies to lease village-owned land. The peasants, in chronic need of ready cash for taxes and foreign consumer goods, were only too willing to lease their land to the foreign companies for very modest sums and under terms dictated by the firms. Where land was still held communally, the village headman was tempted by high cash commissions offered by plantation companies. He would lease the village land even more cheaply than would the individual peasant or, as was frequently the case, sell out the entire village to the company.[14]

The introduction of the plantation meant the divorce of agriculture from nourishment, as the notion of food value was lost to the overriding claim of "market value" in international trade. Crops such as sugar, tobacco, and coffee were selected, not on the basis of how well they feed people, but for their high price value relative to their weight and bulk so that profit margins could be maintained even after the costs of shipping to Europe.

Suppressing Peasant Farming

The stagnation and impoverishment of the peasant food-producing sector was not the mere by-product of benign neglect, that is, the unintended consequence of an overemphasis on export production. Plantations—just like modern "agro-industrial complexes"—needed an abundant and readily available supply of low-wage agricultural workers. Colonial administrations thus devised a variety of tactics, all to undercut self-provisioning agriculture and thus make rural populations dependent on plantation wages. Government services and even the most minimal infrastructure (access to water, roads, seeds, credit, pest and disease control information, and so on) were systematically denied. Plantations usurped most of the good land, either making much of the rural population landless or pushing them onto marginal soils. (Yet the plantations have often held much of their land idle simply to prevent the peasants from using it—even to this day. Del Monte owns 57,000 acres of Guatemala but plants only 9000. The rest lies idle except for a few thousand head of grazing cattle.)[15]

In some cases a colonial administration would go even further to guarantee itself a labor supply. In at least twelve countries in the eastern and southern parts of Africa the exploitation of mineral wealth (gold, diamonds, and copper) and the establishment of cash-crop plantations demanded a continuous supply of low-cost labor. To assure this labor supply, colonial administrations simply expropriated the land of the African communities by violence and drove the people into small reserves.[16] With neither adequate land for their traditional slash-and-burn methods nor access to the means—tools, water, and fertilizer—to make continuous farming of such limited areas viable, the indigenous population could scarcely meet subsistence needs, much less produce surplus to sell in order to cover the colonial taxes. Hundreds of thousands of Africans were forced to become the cheap labor source so "needed" by the colonial plantations. Only by laboring on plantations and in the mines could they hope to pay the colonial taxes.

The tax scheme to produce reserves of cheap plantation and mining labor was particularly effective when the Great Depression hit and the bottom dropped out of cash crop economies. In 1929 the cotton market collapsed, leaving peasant cotton producers, such as those in Upper Volta, unable to pay their colonial taxes. More and more young people, in some years as many as 80,000, were thus forced to migrate to the Gold Coast to compete with each other for low-wage jobs on cocoa plantations.[17]

The forced migration of Africa's most able—bodied workers—stripping village food farming of needed hands—was a recurring feature of colonialism. As late as 1973 the Portuguese "exported" 400,000 Mozambican peasants to work in South Africa in exchange for gold deposited in the Lisbon treasury.

The many techniques of colonialism to undercut self-provisioning agriculture in order to ensure a cheap labor supply are no better illustrated than by the story of how, in the mid-nineteenth century, sugar plantation owners in British Guiana coped with the double blow of the emancipation of slaves and the crash in the world sugar market. The story is graphically recounted by Alan Adamson in *Sugar Without Slaves*.[18]

Would the ex-slaves be allowed to take over the plantation land and grow the food they needed? The planters, many ruined by the sugar slump, were determined they would not. The planter-dominated government devised several schemes for thwarting food self-sufficiency. The price of crown land was kept artificially high, and the purchase of land in parcels smaller than 100 acres was outlawed—two measures guaranteeing that newly organized ex-slave cooperatives could not hope to gain access to much land. The government also prohibited cultivation on as much as 400,000 acres—on the grounds of "uncertain property titles."

Moreover, although many planters held part of their land out of sugar production due to the depressed world price, they would not allow any alternative production on them. They feared that once the ex-slaves started growing food it would be difficult to return them to sugar production when world market prices began to recover. In addition, the government taxed peasant production, then turned around and used the funds to subsidize the immigration of laborers from India and Malaysia to replace the freed slaves, thereby making sugar production again profitable for the planters. Finally, the government neglected the infrastructure for subsistence agriculture and denied credit for small farmers.

Perhaps the most insidious tactic to "lure" the peasant away from food production—and the one with profound historical consequences—was a policy of keeping the price of imported food low through the removal of tariffs and subsidies. The policy was double-edged: first, peasants were told they need not grow food because they could always buy it cheaply with their plantation wages; second, cheap food imports destroyed the market for domestic food and thereby impoverished local food producers.

Adamson relates how both the Governor of British Guiana and the Secretary for the Colonies Earl Grey favored low duties on imports in order to erode local food production and thereby release labor for the plantations. In 1851 the governor rushed through a reduction of the duty on cereals in order to "divert" labor to the sugar estates. As Adamson comments, "Without realizing it, he [the governor] had put his finger on the most mordant feature of monoculture: . . . its convulsive need to destroy any other sector of the economy which might compete for 'its' labor."[19]

Many colonial governments succeeded in establishing dependence on imported foodstuffs. In 1647 an observer in the West Indies wrote to Governor Winthrop of Massachusetts: "Men are so intent upon planting sugar that they had rather buy foode at very deare rates than produce it by labour, so infinite is the profitt of sugar workes . . . "[20] By 1770, the West Indies were importing most of the continental colonies' exports of dried fish, grain, beans, and vegetables. A dependence on imported food made the West Indian colonies vulnerable to any disruption in supply. This dependence on imported food stuffs spelled disaster when the thirteen continental colonies gained independence and food exports from the continent to the West Indies were interrupted. With no diversified food system to fall back on, 15,000 plantation workers died of famine between 1780 and 1787 in Jamaica alone.[21] The dependence of the West Indies on imported food persists to this day.

Suppressing Peasant Competition

We have talked about the techniques by which indigenous populations were forced to cultivate cash crops. In some countries with large plantations, however, colonial governments found it necessary to *prevent* peasants from independently growing cash crops not out of concern for their welfare, but so that they would not compete with colonial interests growing the same crop. For peasant farmers, given a modicum of opportunity, proved themselves capable of outproducing the large plantations not only in terms of output per unit of land but, more important, in terms of capital cost per unit produced.

In the Dutch East Indies (Indonesia and Dutch New Guinea) colonial policy in the middle of the nineteenth century forbade the sugar refineries to buy sugar cane from indigenous growers and imposed a discriminatory tax on rubber produced by native smallholders.[22]

A recent unpublished United Nations study of agricultural development in Africa concluded that large-scale agricultural operations owned and controlled by foreign commercial interests (such as the rubber plantations of Liberia, the sisal estates of Tanganyika [Tanzania], and the coffee estates of Angola) only survived the competition of peasant producers because "the authorities actively supported them by suppressing indigenous rural development."[23]

The suppression of indigenous agricultural development served the interests of the colonizing powers in two ways. Not only did it prevent direct competition from more efficient native producers of the same crops, but it also guaranteed a labor force to work on foreign-owned estates. Planters and foreign investors were not unaware that peasants who could survive economically by their own production would be under less pressure to sell their labor cheaply to the large estates.

The answer to the question, then, "Why can't people feed themselves?" must begin with an understanding of how colonialism actively prevented people from doing just that.

Colonialism

- forced peasants to replace food crops with cash crops that were then expropriated at very low rates;
- took over the best agricultural land for export crop plantations and then forced the most able-bodied workers to leave the village fields to work as slaves or for very low wages on plantations;
- encouraged a dependence on imported food;
- blocked native peasant cash crop production from competing with cash crops produced by settlers or foreign firms.

These are concrete examples of the development of underdevelopment that we should have perceived as such even as we read our history schoolbooks. Why didn't we? Somehow our schoolbooks always seemed to make the flow of history appear to have its own logic—as if it could not have been any other way. I, Frances, recall, in particular, a grade-school, social studies pamphlet on the idyllic life of Pedro, a nine-year-old boy on a coffee plantation in South America. The drawings of lush vegetation and "exotic" huts made his life seem romantic indeed. Wasn't it natural and proper that South America should have plantations to supply my mother and father with coffee? Isn't that the way it was *meant* to be?

Notes

1. Radha Sinha, *Food and Poverty* (New York: Holmes and Meier, 1976), p. 26.
2. John Stuart Mill, *Political Economy*, Book 3, Chapter 25 (emphasis added).
3. Peter Feldman and David Lawrence, "Social and Economic Implications of the Large-Scale Introduction of New Varieties of Foodgrains," Africa Report, preliminary draft (Geneva: UNRISD, 1975), pp.107–108.
4. Edgar Owens, *Right Side of History*, unpublished manuscript, 1976.
5. Walter Rodney, *How Europe Underdeveloped Africa* (London: Bogle-L'Ouverture Publications, 1972), pp. 171–172.
6. Ferdinand Ossendowski, *Slaves of the Sun* (New York: Dutton, 1928), p. 276.
7. Rodney, *How Europe Underdeveloped Africa*, pp. 171–172.
8. Ibid., p. 181.
9. Clifford Geertz, *Agricultural Involution* (Berkeley and Los Angeles: University of California Press, 1963), pp. 52–53.
10. Rodney, *How Europe Underdeveloped Africa*, p. 185.
11. Ibid., p. 184.
12. Ibid., p. 186.
13. George L. Beckford, *Persistent Poverty: Underdevelopment in Plantation Economies of the Third World* (New York: Oxford University Press, 1972), p. 99.
14. Ibid., p. 99, quoting from Erich Jacoby, *Agrarian Unrest in Southeast Asia* (New York: Asia Publishing House, 1961), p. 66.
15. Pat Flynn and Roger Burbach, North American Congress on Latin America, Berkeley, California, recent investigation.
16. Feldman and Lawrence, "Social and Economic Implications," p. 103.
17. Special Sahelian Office Report, Food and Agriculture Organization, March 28,1974, pp. 88–89.
18. Alan Adamson, *Sugar Without Slaves:The Political Economy of British Guiana*, 1838–1904 (New Haven and London: Yale University Press, 1972).

Globalization and Inequality

Joseph Stiglitz

Joseph Stiglitz (b. 1943) is an American economist and a professor at Columbia University. A former chief economist at the World Bank, he won the Nobel Prize for Economics in 2001.

Globalism's Discontents

Few subjects have polarized people throughout the world as much as globalization. Some see it as the way of the future, bringing unprecedented prosperity to everyone, everywhere. Others, symbolized by the Seattle protestors of December 1999, fault globalization as the source of untold problems, from the destruction of native cultures to increasing poverty and immiseration. In this [chapter], I want to sort out the different meanings of globalization. In many countries, globalization has brought huge benefits to a few with few benefits to the many. But in the case of a few countries, it has brought enormous benefit to the many. Why have there been these huge differences in experiences? The answer is that globalization has meant different things in different places.

The countries that have managed globalization on their own, such as those in East Asia, have, by and large, ensured that they reaped huge benefits and that those benefits were equitably shared; they were able substantially to control the terms on which they engaged with the global economy. By contrast, the countries that have, by and large, had globalization managed for them by the International Monetary Fund (IMF) and other international economic institutions have not done so well. The problem is thus not with globalization but with how it has been managed.

The international financial institutions have pushed a particular ideology—market fundamentalism—that is both bad economics and bad politics; it is based on premises concerning how markets work that do not hold even for developed countries, much less for developing countries. The IMF has pushed these economics policies without a broader vision of society or the role of economics within society. And it has pushed these policies in ways that have undermined emerging democracies.

More generally, globalization itself has been governed in ways that are undemocratic and have been disadvantageous to developing countries, especially the poor within those countries. The Seattle protestors pointed to the absence of democracy and of transparency, the governance of the international economic institutions by and for special corporate and financial interests, and the absence of countervailing democratic checks to ensure that these informal and *public* institutions serve a general interest. In these complaints, there is more than a grain of truth.

Beneficial Globalization

Of the countries of the world, those in East Asia have grown the fastest and done most to reduce poverty. And they have done so, emphatically, via "globalization." Their growth has been based on exports—by taking advantage of the global market for exports and by closing the technology gap. It was not just gaps in capital and other resources that separated the developed from the less-developed countries, but differences in knowledge. East Asian countries took advantage of the "globalization of knowledge" to reduce these disparities. But while some of the countries in the region grew by opening themselves up to multinational companies, others, such as Korea and Taiwan, grew by creating their own enterprises. Here is the key distinction: Each of the most successful globalizing countries determined its own pace of change; each made sure as it grew that the benefits were shared equitably; each rejected the basic tenets of the "Washington Consensus," which argued for a minimalist role for government and rapid privatization and liberalization.

In East Asia, government took an active role in managing the economy. The steel industry that the Korean government created was among the most efficient in the world—performing far better than its private-sector rivals in the United States (which, though private, are constantly turning to the government for protection and for subsidies). Financial markets were highly regulated. My research shows that those regulations promoted growth. It was only when these countries stripped away the regulations, under pressure from the U.S. Treasury and the IMF, that they encountered problems.

During the 1960s, 1970s, and 1980s, the East Asian economies not only grew rapidly but were remarkably stable. Two of the countries most touched by the 1997–1998 economic crisis had had in the preceding three decades not a single year of negative growth; two had only one year—a better performance than the United States or the other wealthy nations that make up the Organization for Economic Cooperation and Development (OECD). The single most important factor leading to the troubles that several of the East Asian countries encountered in the late 1990s—the East Asian crisis—was the rapid liberalization of financial and capital markets. In short, the countries of East Asia benefited from globalization because they made globalization work for them; it was when they succumbed to the pressures from the outside that they ran into problems that were beyond their own capacity to manage well.

Globalization can yield immense benefits. Elsewhere in the developing world, globalization of knowledge has brought improved health, with life spans increasing at a rapid pace. How can one put a price on these benefits of globalization? Globalization has brought still other benefits: Today there is the beginning of a globalized civil society that has begun to succeed with such reforms as the Mine Ban Treaty and debt forgiveness for the poorest highly indebted countries (the Jubilee movement). The globalization protest movement itself would not have been possible without globalization.

The Darker Side of Globalization

How then could a trend with the power to have so many benefits have produced such opposition? Simply because it has not only failed to live up to its potential but frequently has had very adverse effects. But this forces us to ask, why has it had such adverse effects? The answer can be seen by looking at each of the economic elements of globalization as pursued by the international financial institutions and especially by the IMF.

The most adverse effects have arisen from the liberalization of financial and capital markets—which has posed risks to developing countries without commensurate rewards. The liberalization has left them prey to hot money pouring into the country, an influx that has fueled speculative real-estate booms; just as suddenly, as investor sentiment changes, the money is pulled out, leaving in its wake economic devastation. Early on, the IMF said that these countries were being rightly punished for pursuing bad economic policies. But as the crisis spread from country to country, even those that the IMF had given high marks found themselves ravaged.

The IMF often speaks about the importance of the discipline by capital markets. In doing so, it exhibits a certain paternalism, a new form of the old colonial mentality: "We in the establishment, we in the North who run our capital markets, know best. Do what we tell you to do, and you will prosper." The arrogance is offensive, but the objection is more than just to style. The position is highly undemocratic: There is an implied assumption that democracy by itself does not provide sufficient discipline. But if one is to have an external disciplinarian, one should choose a good disciplinarian who knows what is good for growth, who shares one's values. One doesn't want an arbitrary and capricious taskmaster who one moment praises you for your values and the next screams at you for being rotten to the core. But capital markets are just such a fickle taskmaster; even ardent advocates talk about their bouts of irrational exuberance followed by equally irrational pessimism.

Lessons of Crisis

Nowhere was the fickleness more evident than in the last global financial crisis. Historically, most of the disturbances in capital flows into and out of a country are not the result of factors inside the country. Major disturbances arise, rather, from influences outside the country. When Argentina suddenly faced high interest rates in 1998, it wasn't because of what Argentina did but because of what happened in Russia. Argentina cannot be blamed for Russia's crisis.

Small developing countries find it virtually impossible to withstand this volatility. I have described capital-market liberalization with a simple metaphor: Small countries are like small boats. Liberalizing capital markets is like setting them loose on a rough sea. Even if the boats are well captained, even if the boats are sound, they are likely to be hit broadside by a big wave and capsize. But the IMF pushed for the boats to set forth into the roughest parts of the sea before they were seaworthy, with untrained captains and crews, and without life vests. No wonder matters turned out so badly!

To see why it is important to choose a disciplinarian who shares one's values, consider a world in which there were free mobility of skilled labor. Skilled labor would then provide discipline. Today, a country that does not treat capital well will find capital quickly withdrawing; in a world of free labor mobility, if a country did not treat skilled labor well, it too would withdraw. Workers would worry about the quality of their children's education and their family's health care, the quality of their environment and of their own wages and working conditions. They would say to the government: If you fail to provide these essentials, we will move elsewhere. That is a far cry from the kind of discipline that free-flowing capital provides.

The liberalization of capital markets has not brought growth: How can one build factories or create jobs with money that can come in and out of a country overnight? And it gets worse: Prudential behavior requires countries to set aside reserves equal to the amount of short-term lending; so if a firm in a poor country borrows $100 million at, say, 20 percent interest rates short-term from a bank in the United States, the government must set aside a corresponding amount. The reserves are typically held in U.S. Treasury bills—a safe, liquid asset. In effect, the country is borrowing $100 million from the United States and lending $100 million to the United States. But when it borrows, it pays a high interest rate, 20 percent; when it lends, it receives a low interest rate, around 4 percent. This may be great for the United States, but it can hardly help the growth of the poor country. There is also a high *opportunity* cost of the reserves; the money could have been much better spent on building rural roads or constructing schools or health clinic. But instead, the country is, in effect, forced to lend money to the United States.

Thailand illustrates the true ironies of such policies: There, the free market led to investments in empty office buildings, starving other sectors—such as education and transportation—of badly needed resources. Until the IMF and the U.S. Treasury came along, Thailand had restricted bank lending for speculative real estate. The Thais had seen the record: Such lending is an essential part of the boom-bust cycle that has characterized capitalism for 200 years. It wanted to be sure that the scarce capital went to create jobs. But the IMF nixed this intervention in the free market. If the free market said, "Build empty office buildings," so be it! The market knew better than any government bureaucrat who mistakenly might have thought it wiser to build schools or factories.

The Costs of Volatility

Capital-market liberalization is inevitably accompanied by huge volatility, and this volatility impedes growth and increases poverty. It increases the risks of investing in the country, and thus investors demand a risk premium in the form of higher-than-normal profits. Not only is growth not enhanced but poverty is increased through several channels. The high volatility increases the likelihood of recessions—and the poor always bear the brunt of such downturns. Even in developed countries, safety nets are weak or nonexistent among the selfemployed and in the rural sector. But these are the dominant sectors in developing countries. Without adequate safety nets, the recessions that follow from capital-market liberalization lead to impoverishment. In the name of imposing budget discipline and reassuring investors, the IMF invariably demands expenditure reductions, which almost inevitably result in cuts in outlays for safety nets that are already threadbare.

But matters are even worse—for under the doctrines of the "discipline of the capital markets," if countries try to tax capital, capital flees. Thus, the IMF doctrines inevitably lead to an increase in tax burdens on the poor and the middle classes. Thus, while IMF bailouts enable the rich to take their money out of the country at more favorable terms (at the overvalued exchange rates), the burden of repaying the loans lies with the workers who remain behind.

The reason that I emphasize capital-market liberalization is that the case against it—and against the IMF's stance in pushing it—is so compelling. It illustrates what can go wrong with globalization. Even economists like Jagdish Bhagwati, strong advocates of free trade, see the folly in liberalizing capital markets. Belatedly, so too has the IMF—at least in its official rhetoric, though less so in its policy stances—but too late for all those countries that have suffered so much from following the IMF's prescriptions,

But while the case for trade liberalization—when properly done—is quite compelling, the way it has been pushed by the IMF has been far more problematic. The basic logic is simple: Trade liberalization is supposed to result in resources moving from inefficient protected sectors to more efficient export sectors. The problem is not only that job destruction comes before the job creation—so that unemployment and poverty result—but that the IMF's "structural adjustment programs" (designed in ways that allegedly would reassure global investors) make job creation almost impossible. For these programs are often accompanied by high interest rates that are often justified by a single-minded focus on inflation. Sometimes that concern is deserved; often, though, it is carried to an extreme. In the United States, we worry that small increases in the interest rate will discourage investment. The IMF has pushed for far higher interest rates in countries with a far less hospitable investment environment. The high interest rates mean that new jobs and enterprises are not created. What happens is that trade liberalization, rather than moving workers from low-productivity jobs to high-productivity ones, moves them from low-productivity jobs to unemployment. Rather than enhanced growth, the effect is increased poverty. To make matters worse, the unfair trade-liberalization agenda forces poor countries to compete with highly subsidized American and European agriculture. . . .

An Unfair Trade Agenda

The trade-liberalization agenda has been set by the North, or more accurately, by special interests in the North. Consequently, a disproportionate part of the gains has accrued to the advanced industrial countries, and in some cases the less-developed countries have actually been worse off. After the last round of trade negotiations, the Uruguay Round that ended in 1994, the World Bank calculated the gains and losses to each of the regions of the world. The United States and Europe gained enormously. But sub-Saharan Africa, the poorest region of the world, lost by about 2 percent because of terms-of-trade effects: The trade negotiations opened their markets to manufactured goods produced by the industrialized countries but did not open up the markets of Europe and the United States to the agricultural goods in which poor countries often have a comparative advantage. Nor did the trade agreements eliminate the subsidies to agriculture that make it so hard for the developing countries to compete.

The U.S. negotiations with China over its membership in the WTO displayed a double standard bordering on the surreal. The U.S. trade representative, the chief negotiator for the United States, began by insisting that China was a developed country. Under WTO rules, developing countries are allowed longer transition periods in which state subsidies and other departures from the WTO strictures are permitted. China certainly wishes it were a developed country, with Western-style per capita incomes. And since China has a lot of "capitas," it's possible to multiply a huge number of people by very small average incomes and conclude that the People's Republic is a big economy. But China is not only a developing economy; it is a low-income developing country. Yet the United States insisted that China be treated like a developed country! China went along with the fiction; the negotiations dragged on so long that China got some extra time to adjust. But the true hypocrisy was shown when U.S. negotiators asked, in effect, for developing-country status for the United States to get extra time to shelter the American textile industry.

Trade negotiations in the service industries also illustrate the unlevel nature of the playing field. Which service industries did the United States say were *very* important? Financial services—industries in which Wall Street has a comparative advantage. Construction industries and maritime services were not on the agenda, because the developing countries would have a comparative advantage in these sectors.

Consider also intellectual-property rights, which are important if innovators are to have incentives to innovate (though many of the corporate advocates of intellectual property exaggerate its importance and fail to note that much of the most important research, as in basic science and mathematics, is not patentable). Intellectual-property rights, such as patents and trademarks, need to balance the interests of producers with those of users—not only users in developing countries, but researchers in developed countries.

If we underprice the profitability of innovation to the inventor, we deter invention. If we overprice its cost to the research community and the end user, we retard its diffusion and beneficial effects on living standards.

In the final stages of the Uruguay negotiations, both the White House Office of Science and Technology Policy and the Council of Economic Advisers worried that we had not got the balance right—that the agreement put producers' interests over users'. We worried that, with this imbalance, the rate of progress and innovation might actually be impeded. After all, knowledge is the most important input into research, and overly strong intellectual-property rights can, in effect, increase the price of this input. We were also concerned about the consequences of denying life-saving medicines to the poor. This issue subsequently gained international attention in the context of the provision of AIDS medicines in South Africa. The international outrage forced the drug companies to back down—and it appears that, going forward, the most adverse consequences will be circumscribed. But it is worth noting that initially, even the Democratic U.S. administration supported the pharmaceutical companies.

What we were not fully aware of was another danger—what has come to be called "biopiracy," which involves international drug companies patenting traditional medicines. Not only do they seek to make money from "resources" and knowledge that rightfully belong to the developing countries, but in doing so they squelch domestic firms who long provided these traditional medicines. While it is not clear whether these patents would hold up in court if they were effectively challenged, it is clear that the less-developed countries may not have the legal and financial resources required to mount such a challenge. The issue has become the source of enormous emotional, and potentially economic, concern throughout the developing world. This fall, while I was in Ecuador visiting a village in the high Andes, the Indian mayor railed against how globalization had led to biopiracy. . . .

Trickle-Down Economics

We recognize today that there is a "social contract" that binds citizens together, and with their government. When government policies abrogate that social contract, citizens may not honor their "contracts" with each other, or with the government. Maintaining that social contract is particularly important, and difficult, in the midst of the social upheavals that so frequently accompany the development transformation. In the green eye-shaded calculations of the IMF macro-economics there is, too often, no room for these concerns.

Part of the social contract entails "fairness," that the poor share in the gains of society as it grows, and that the rich share in the pains of society in times of crisis. The Washington Consensus policies paid little attention to issues of distribution or "fairness." If pressed, many of its proponents would argue that the best way to help the poor is to make the economy grow. They believe in trickle-down economics. *Eventually*, it is asserted, the benefits of that growth *trickle down* even to the poor. Trickle-down economics was never much more than just a belief, an article of faith. Pauperism seemed to grow in nineteenth-century England even though the country as a whole prospered. Growth in America in the 1980s provided the most recent dramatic example: while the economy grew, those at the bottom saw their real incomes decline. The Clinton administration had argued strongly against trickle-down economics; it believed that there had to be active programs to help the poor. And when I left the White House to go to the World Bank, I brought with me the same skepticism of trickle-down economics; if this had not worked in the United States, why would it work in developing countries? While it is true that sustained reductions in poverty cannot be attained without robust economic growth, the converse is not true: growth need not benefit all. It is not true that "a rising tide lifts all boats." Sometimes, a quickly rising tide, especially when accompanied by a storm, dashes weaker boats against the shore, smashing them to smithereens.

In spite of the obvious problems confronting trickle-down economics, it has a good intellectual pedigree. One Nobel Prize winner, Arthur Lewis, argued that inequality was good for development and economic growth, since the rich save more than the poor, and the key to growth was capital accumulation. Another Nobel

Prize winner, Simon Kuznets, argued that while in the initial stages of development inequality increased, later on the trend was reversed.[1]

The history of the past fifty years has, however, not supported these theories and hypotheses. East Asian countries—South Korea, China, Taiwan, Japan—showed that high savings did not require high inequality, that one could achieve rapid growth without a substantial increase in inequality. Because the governments did not believe that growth would automatically benefit the poor, and because they believed that greater *equality* would actually enhance growth, governments in the region took active steps to ensure that the rising tide of growth did lift most boats, that wage inequalities were kept in bounds, that some educational opportunity was extended to all. Their policies led to social and political stability, which in turn contributed to an economic environment in which businesses flourished. Tapping new reservoirs of talent provided the energy and human skills that contributed to the dynamism of the region.

Elsewhere, where governments adopted the Washington Consensus policies, the poor have benefited less from growth. In Latin America, growth has not been accompanied by a reduction in inequality, or even a reduction in poverty. In some cases poverty has actually increased, as evidenced by the urban slums that dot the landscape. The IMF talks with pride about the progress Latin America has made in market reforms over the past decade (though somewhat more quietly after the collapse of the star student Argentina in 2001, and the recession and stagnation that have afflicted many of the "reform" countries during the past five years), but has said less about the numbers in poverty.

Clearly, growth alone does not always improve the lives of all a country's people. Not surprisingly, the phrase "trickle-down" has disappeared from the policy debate. But, in a slightly mutated form, the idea is still alive. I call the new variant *trickle-down-plus*. It holds that growth is necessary and *almost* sufficient for reducing poverty—implying that the best strategy is simply to focus on growth, while mentioning issues like female education and health. But proponents of trickle-down-plus failed to implement policies that would effectively address either broader concerns of poverty or even specific issues such as the education of women. In practice, the advocates of trickle-down-plus continued with much the same policies as before, with much the same adverse effects. The overly stringent "adjustment policies" in country after country forced cutbacks in education and health: in Thailand, as a result, not only did female prostitution increase but expenditures on AIDS were cut way back; and what had been one of the world's most successful programs in fighting AIDS had a major setback.

The irony was that one of the major proponents of trickle-down-plus was the U.S. Treasury under the Clinton administration. Within the administration, in domestic politics, there was a wide spectrum of views, from New Democrats, who wanted to see a more limited role for government, to Old Democrats, who looked for more government intervention. But the central view, reflected in the annual Economic Report of the President (prepared by the Council of Economic Advisers), argued strongly against trickle-down economics—or even trickle-down-plus. Here was the U.S. Treasury pushing policies on other countries that, had they been advocated for the United States, would have been strongly contested *within the administration,* and almost surely defeated. The reason for this seeming inconsistency was simple: The IMF and the World Bank were part of Treasury's turf, an arena in which, with few exceptions, they were allowed to push their perspectives, just as other departments, within their domains, could push theirs. . . .

Global Social Justice

Today, in much of the developing world, globalization is being questioned. For instance, in Latin America, after a short burst of growth in the early 1990s, stagnation and recession have set in. The growth was not sustained—some might say, was not sustainable. Indeed, at this juncture, the growth record of the so-called post-reform era looks no better, and in some countries much worse, than in the widely criticized import-substitution period of the 1950s and 1960s when Latin countries tried to industrialize by discouraging imports. Indeed, reform critics point out that the burst of growth in the early 1990s was little more than a "catch-up" that did not even make up for the lost decade of the 1980s.

Throughout the region, people are asking: "Has reform failed or has globalization failed?" The distinction is perhaps artificial, for globalization was at the center of the reforms. Even in those countries that have managed to grow, such as Mexico, the benefits have accrued largely to the upper 30 percent and have been even more concentrated in the top 10 percent. Those at the bottom have gained little; many are even worse off. The reforms have exposed countries to greater risk, and the risks have been borne disproportionately by those least able to cope with them. Just as in many countries where the pacing and sequencing of reforms has resulted in job destruction outmatching job creation, so too has the exposure to risk outmatched the ability to create institutions for coping with risk, including effective safety nets.

In this bleak landscape, there are some positive signs. Those in the North have become more aware of the inequities of the global economic architecture. The agreement at Doha to hold a new round of trade negotiations—the "Development Round"—promises to rectify some of the imbalances of the past. There has been a marked change in the rhetoric of the international economic institutions—at least they talk about poverty. At the World Bank, there have been some real reforms; there has been some progress in translating the rhetoric into reality—in ensuring that the voices of the poor are heard and the concerns of the developing countries are listened to. But elsewhere, there is often a gap between the rhetoric and the reality. Serious reforms in governance, in who makes decisions and how they are made, are not on the table. If one of the problems at the IMF has been that the ideology, interests, and perspectives of the financial community in the advanced industrialized countries have been given disproportionate weight (in matters whose effects go well beyond finance), then the prospects for success in the current discussions of reform, in which the same parties continue to predominate, are bleak. They are more likely to result in slight changes in the shape of the table, not changes in who is *at* the table or what is on the agenda.

September 11 has resulted in a global alliance against terrorism. What we now need is not just an alliance *against* evil, but an alliance *for* something positive—a global alliance for reducing poverty and for creating a better environment, an alliance for creating a global society with more social justice.

NOTE

1. See W. A. Lewis, "Economic Development with Unlimited Supplies of Labor." *Manchester School* 22 (1954), pp. 139–91, and S. Kuznets, "Economic Growth and Income Inequality," *American Economic Review* 45(1) (1955), pp. 1–28.

The New Global American Dilemma and Terrorism

Fathali M. Moghaddam

Georgetown University

KEY WORDS: American dilemma, Terrorism, Degrees of freedom, Fractured globalization, Catastrophic evolution

The "New Global American Dilemma" and Terrorism

Psychological research on terrorism suffers from two main weaknesses, both of which arise from well known weaknesses in mainstream psychology (Moghaddam, 2005a). The first weakness is a lack of powerful conceptual frameworks, and a reductionist-positivist reliance on data gathering on the assumption that data will allow us to mimic the success of the "real sciences" such as physics, and "real scientists" such as Einstein. Seldom have we bothered to notice that Einstein carried out thought experiments, not laboratory experiments. Of course experiments yielding data are needed, but there has to be a corresponding development in powerful theories.

Psychology journals have produced mountains of "data" about individual difference measures, and particularly since 9/11 we are drowning in oceans of information about terrorists (there is now an international "terrorism studies industry" generating more data than anyone can possibly keep up with); what we lack are conceptual frameworks powerful enough to interpret this information. The concept of *significance quest*, "an overarching motive propelling suicide terrorism" (Kruglanski, Chen. Deshesne, Fishman, & Orchek, 2009. p. 335), is integrative and potentially very useful in helping us interpret some of the information being accumulated on terrorism.

A second weakness of mainstream psychology is a tendency for researchers to split into "dispositional" and "contextual" camps, each camp supporting a competing picture of behavior as shaped by individual differences or contextual factors. Underlying this debate is the assumption that the contribution of dispositional and contextual factors is fixed. An alternative and more accurate viewpoint is to treat the role of both dispositional and contextual factors as variable. The role of cultural context in shaping individual behavior is not static; rather, this role varies considerably across time and space. Presumably, the role and nature of a significance quest in relation to terrorism is also variable; this is an idea that needs further development.

My treatment of "context" is macro: a significance quest and terrorism should be assessed in the context of evolutionary transformations and globalization (Moghaddam, 2008a). In part one, I explore the varying role of cultural context through the concept of "degrees of freedom" (Moghaddam, 2005a). At present, the context of some of the most influential Islamic communities in terms of radical Islamic ideology, such as in Iraq, Afghanistan. Saudi Arabia, and the tribal regions of Pakistan, is characterized by low degrees of freedom, rendering dispositional characteristics of less relevance toward understanding terrorism. The implication is that in present circumstances, terrorism emanating from some Islamic communities can best be understood through analysis of contextual characteristics, rather than attention to "individual difference" variables. However, it is possible that circumstances will change and render individual difference factors of greater importance in the understanding of future Islamic terrorism.

In part two, I argue that we must also consider the macro global and evolutionary context of a significance quest and its relation to contemporary Islamic terrorism. From this viewpoint, Islamic terrorism is a "defense mechanism," albeit a dysfunctional one, adopted by fundamentalist groups who feel threatened by globalization. The experience of threat and relative deprivation among traditional and fundamentalist Muslims arises in the context of rapid "fractured" globalization, with its associated contradictions. Among the most important of such contradictions is the *New Global American Dilemma*, which arises from the enormous gap between American ideals and American practices in the realm of foreign policy. This is the main topic of the third part of the discussion.

Thus, while I see the concept of the significance quest as very useful, I argue that this concept should be applied to terrorism within the macro context in which Islamic terrorism is taking place, because under current circumstances it is the context, and not the characteristics of individuals, that determines terrorist actions. By focusing on the context, I am also highlighting the situation "from the terrorists' point of view" (Moghaddam, 2006a), rather than the point of view of "outsiders" who view terrorist actions and attribute responsibility to individuals. A parallel contrast exists in the realm of torture: between those who view torture in places such as Abu Ghraib prison as arising out of the characteristics of certain contexts, and others who point to "a few bad apples" as the reason for torture (Moghaddam, 2007).

Degrees of Freedom and the Varying Power of Context

A long-standing debate in research on human behavior is the relative contributions of dispositional and contextual factors (Moghaddam, 2005a). A continued criticism of mainstream research is that it has been unduly influenced by the "individualism" of American culture and adopted reductionist accounts, in line with a "self-help" capitalist ideology (e.g., Hepburn, 2003). This criticism is accurate in so far as American psychology has for many decades constituted the "First World" of modern psychology and American values have permeated mainstream psychological research (Moghaddam. 1987), but the criticism is misguided in treating the influence of contextual (and disposition) factors as static. The concept of "degrees of freedom" helps to clarify this issue, and I will discuss this concept using the metaphor of a staircase to terrorism (Moghaddam. 2005b).

Consider a multistory building with a winding staircase at its center. People are located on different floors of the building, but everyone begins on the ground floor, where there are over a billion Muslims. Thought and action on each floor are characterized by particular psychological processes. On the ground floor, the most important psychological processes influencing behavior are psychological interpretations of material conditions, perceptions of fairness, and adequacy of identity. Hundreds of millions of Muslims suffer fraternal deprivation and lack of adequate identity; they feel that they are not being treated fairly and are not receiving adequate material rewards. They feel dissatisfied with the way they are depicted by the international media, and they do not want to become second-class copies of Western ideals. However, on the ground floor, degrees of freedom are large relative to degrees of freedom on the higher floors of the staircase to terrorism, and individual Muslims on the ground floor have a wider range of behavioral options.

Some individuals move up from the ground floor to the first floor, in search of ways to improve their life conditions. These individuals in no way see themselves as terrorists or even supportive of terrorist causes; they are simply attempting to feel better about themselves and to improve their situation. On this floor they are particularly influenced by possibilities for individual mobility and voice. Some of these individuals climb up to the second floor of the staircase, where they come under the influence of persuasive messages telling them that the root cause of their problems is external enemies, spearheaded by America. Individuals on the second floor are encouraged to displace aggression onto external targets.

Many of the individuals who climb up to the second floor of the staircase remain there, but some keep climbing up to reach the third floor where they adopt a morality supportive of terrorism. Gradually, those who have reached the third floor become divorced from the mainstream morality of their society, which generally condemns terrorism (this is also true in Islamic communities), and take on a morality that accepts that "the ends justify the means." Those individuals who continue the climb up to the fourth floor adopt a more rigid style of categorical "us against them," "good against evil" thinking. The world is now unambiguously divided up into "black and white," and it is seen as legitimate to attack "the forces of evil" in any and every way feasible. Some of these individuals move up to the fifth floor, where they take part in and directly support terrorist actions.

The higher individuals move up the staircase to terrorism, the lower the degrees of freedom. In other words, the power of the context increases, and the behavioral options decrease, on the higher floors. After an individual has become part of a terrorist group or network and has reached the highest floor, the only options left open are to try to kill or be killed or captured. Personality factors are less influential, and the context is all-powerful, on the highest floor. In contrast, on the lowest floors the degrees of freedom are greater, meaning that individuals have a wider variety of behavioral options and personality factors potentially play a larger role in who climbs up the staircase.

The significance quest subsumes personal causes, ideological reasons, and social pressures that influence suicide terrorism. The influence of these factors will vary on the different levels of the staircase to terrorism. For example, social pressure will increase (and degrees of freedom diminish) as the individual climbs up the staircase to higher floors. Individual differences regarding personal causes and commitment to ideological causes will be greater on the lowest levels of the staircase. The individuals who have moved up to the highest floors of the staircase to terrorism will be more similar to one another in that they experience far greater social pressure, and the ideological reasons leading them to be involved in terrorism will be more similar. However, very different personal causes might lead people to the higher floors of the staircase.

The New Global American Dilemma

In interpreting suicide terrorism as an extreme case of significance quest, "an opportunity to catapult oneself to the pinnacle of cultural veneration by an act of supreme sacrifice for an ideologically touted cause," Kruglanski et al. (2009, pp. 337–338) have rightly highlighted the cultural conditions which give rise to suicide terrorism. However, there is a bigger picture to consider. The cultural conditions of Muslim societies have not evolved in a vacuum. Rather, they have evolved in an international political order where a twentieth-century rivalry between the Soviet Union and the United States eventually resulted in the United States dominating the world stage as the sole superpower at the start of the twenty-first century. In this new role, the United States faces major dilemmas.

The reductionist nature of modern psychology has resulted in a focus on dilemmas as situated in isolated minds, rather than as imbedded in the normative system shared by a collective (Billig, Condor, Edwards, & Gane, 1988). The alternative, more social approach to considering dilemmas is demonstrated in the research of the Swedish researcher Gunnar Myrdal (1898–1987), who discussed a dilemma confronting American society in the domain of race relations in his seminal study *An American Dilemma* (1944). According to Myrdal, the United States faced a dilemma because on the one hand foundational American documents (e.g., Declaration of Independence, The Federalist Papers, Constitution) claim that all humans are created equal and have the same rights to life, liberty, and the pursuit of happiness, but on the other hand even after the official end of slavery, racial segregation and discrimination continued in America.

The "American dilemma" identified by Myrdal did not reside in isolated American minds. Rather, this dilemma arose out of contradictions between two competing, collectively shared story lines. A first story line positions the United States as the "land of the free" and a place where everyone enjoys equality of opportunity. A second, equally powerful story line positions the United States as a segregated society, where group-based inequalities and discrimination are the norm. Both story lines are collaboratively constructed and collectively upheld by Americans. Myrdal argued, and history proved him to be correct, that the dilemma arising out of these two competing story lines would have to be resolved. The Civil Rights movement and desegregation legislation represent the official resolution of this "first" American dilemma.

But now the United States is confronted by a *new global American dilemma,* one arising out of two competing story lines at the global level. On the one hand, successive United States administrations have espoused that democracy and freedom are the rights of all human beings in all societies. Indeed, the invasion of Iraq by American led forces in 2003 was explained in terms of a "spreading democracy" mandate by the George W. Bush administration. On the other hand, the United States government has continued to support so-called "pro-American" dictatorships in a number of major Islamic societies, including Saudi Arabia and Egypt. This new global American dilemma is keenly felt in Islamic societies, where it is interpreted on the streets as "American hypocrisy."

Following Myrdal's (1944) logic, I have argued that the new global American dilemma will eventually be revolved through American support for democracy, even in the Near and Middle East (Moghaddam, 2008c). However, this dilemma will take decades to resolve, and in the meantime one of its consequences is the creation of conditions in which the radicalization of Muslim communities is more likely. This is because dictatorships in the Near and Middle East continue to crush secular prodemocracy opposition movements, leaving the mosque as the only space in which there is any possibility for collective antigovernment action. The result has been the religious monopoly of political activity and the rise of organizations such as the Muslim Brotherhood and Hizb ut-Tahrir in North Africa and Muslim Asia. Moreover, this radicalization has spilled over to Western Europe, as Muslim immigrants continue to identify with the "troubles" in the Middle East and displace aggression onto Israel and the United States.

It is in the context of the European Union that the need for making a stronger explicit link between significance quest and identity becomes clear. Various identity theories highlight the human motivation to achieve a positive and distinct identity, to be both favorably evaluated and different (see Moghaddam, 2008a, chap. 5). A question arises in the European context, where in practice "home grown" Islamic terrorism has been a greater threat than in the United States: Why is it that terrorism is more likely to represent an example of significance quest in Europe than in the United States? One way to tackle this question is through reference to the "distance traveled hypothesis" (Moghaddam, 2008b): Muslims require less material and "intellectual" (e.g., education level) resources to reach Europe than to reach the United States, and fewer resources mean that they are less able to integrate into the adopted land. Further discussion is needed as to how significance quest is associated with resources and how such relationships influence identity and identification.

Thus, in the global context, it is impossible to make sense of a "significance quest" on the part of Muslims without first appreciating the perceived role of the United States in the continuation of dictatorships in so-called "pro-American" Muslim countries. But we should go even further in widening the scope and assessing terrorism in broader time and space perspectives.

Fractured Globalization, Catastrophic Evolution, and Islamic Terrorism

In this final part of the discussion my goal is to place the significance quest in the wider global and evolutionary context. What aspects of the wider context lead to a significance quest associated with suicide terrorism? I focus on the ways in which globalization and cultural evolution are taking place.

Globalization is taking place in a "fractured" manner, one aspect of which is the coming into contact of groups with little "preadaptation" (Moghaddam, 2006). This "sudden contact" has resulted in catastrophic evolution, the rapid decline or even extinction of one or both groups making contact. The phenomenon of catastrophic evolution is well known in environmental studies and documented in declining diversity among animals and plants (e.g., see Ehrlich & Ehrlich, 2008). But the implications of this evolutionary perspective need to be critically considered in more detail.

Sudden contact has been made possible through rapid advances in human transportation and communications systems. These advances have enabled groups of humans to "suddenly show up" on the doorstep of outgroups with which they have no previous history of large-scale contact. The history of Western colonization of Africa and Asia provides endless examples of this process, as well as its consequences. When Columbus arrived in North America, there existed about 15,000 languages in the world, but there are only about 6,000 still alive today, and most of these will be extinct by the end of the twenty-first century (Crystal, 2000). Numerous indigenous African, American, Australian, and Asian cultures and religions have disappeared, as is well known. What is less discussed is the defense mechanisms adopted by groups that face extinction.

Terrorism is a (dysfunctional) defense mechanism adopted by Islamic fundamentalists who perceive their way of life to be under threat and who view expanding westernization as representing a serious threat of extinction for them (Moghaddam, 2008b). The "significance quest" is not just an individual attempt at making oneself supremely significant, but part of a collective strategy adopted by a people who see the real possibility of extinction facing them. My personal experiences of interacting with radical Muslims in Iran prior to the 1978 revolution is that they saw themselves in a life and death struggle against the westernization movement spearheaded by the "American puppet" Shah. Khomeini's victory in Iran was seen by the Islamic fundamentalists as their lifeline to survival, against the "massive onslaught" of American influence. Exactly the same "life and death struggle" is being played out in Muslin communities around the world, with fundamentalists fighting for the survival of their way of life.

Terrorism is only one manifestation of the "significance quest." Various "sacred carriers" (Moghaddam, 2008b), such as the Islamic veil, are also being used as defense mechanisms in this ongoing struggle. Sacred carriers serve to propagate the values and beliefs of a group, an example being the United States national flag, "Old Glory." Like the Islamic veil, a national flag is "just a piece of cloth," but this piece of cloth can take on great importance in the significance quest.

Concluding Comment

Finally, a word of caution about typology is needed. Kruglanski el al. (2009) focus on suicide terrorism, but it is useful to also consider the various other specialties in terrorist networks. The suicide terrorist is an example of a terrorist specialization I term "fodder"; through an analysis of available evidence I have identified eight other specializations in terrorist networks (Moghaddam, 2006, chap. 8). These additional specializations include "source of inspiration," "strategist," "networker," "expert," "cell manager," "local agitator and guide," "local cell member," and "fund raiser." The significance quest is likely to be different in nature for many of these different specialist terrorist types.

Acknowledgments

Correspondence concerning this article should be addressed to Fathali M. Moghaddam. Department of Psychology, White Gravenor Hall (3rd floor), Georgetown University, Washington, D.C., 20057. Email: moghaddf@georgetown.edu

References

Billing, M., Condor, S., Edwards. D., & Gane, M. (1988). *Ideological dilemmas: A social psychology of everyday thinking.* London: Sage.

Crystal, D. (2000). *Language death.* Cambridge: Cambridge University press.

Ehrlich, P. R., & Ehrlich, A. H. (2008). *The dominant animal: Human evolution and the environment.* Washington, DC: Island Press.

Hepburn, A. (2003). *Critical social psychology.* London: Sage.

Kruglanski, A. W., Chen, X., Dechesne, M., Fishman, S., & Orehek, E. (2009). Fully committed: Suicide bombers' motivation and the quest for personal significance. *Political Psychology, 30,* 331–357.

Moghaddam, F. M. (1987). Psychology in the three worlds: As reflected by the "crisis" in social and the move toward indigenous third world psychology. *American Psychologist, 47,* 912–920.

Moghaddam, F. M. (2005a). *Great ideas in psychology.* Oxford: Oneworld.

Moghaddam, F. M. (2005b). The staircase to terrorism: A psychological exploration. *American Psychologist, 60,* 161–169.

Moghaddam, F. M. (2006a). *From the terrorists' point of view.* Westport, CT: Praeger.

Moghaddam, F. M. (2006b). Catastrophic evolution, culture and diversity management policy. *Culture & Psychology, 12,* 415–434.

Moghaddam, F. M. (2007). Interrogation policy and American psychology in global context. *Journal of Peace Psychology, 13,* 437–443.

Moghaddam. F. M. (2008a). *Multiculturalism and intergroup relations.* Washington, DC: American Psychological Association Press.

Moghaddam, F. M. (2008b). *How globalization spurs terrorism.* Wesport, CT: Praeger.

Moghaddam, F. M. (2008c). *Violent Islamist extremism in global context.* Prepared statement presented before the United States Senate Committee on Homeland Security and Governmental Affairs, July 10, 2008.

Myrdal, G. (1944). *An American dilemma: The Negro problem and modern democracy.* (2 vols). New York: Harper and Bothers.